It's NEVER About The Money... even when it is

How to Untangle Your Emotions From Your Money

Pegi Burdick
THE FINANCIAL WHISPERER®

It's NEVER About The Money... Even When It Is
How to Untangle Your Emotions From Your Money

Copyright © 2012 by Pegi Burdick

All rights reserved. No part of this publication may be reproduced or transmitted in any form or by any means, electronic or mechanical, including photocopy, recording, or any information storage and retrieval system, without permission in writing from the publisher.

Requests for permission to make copies of any part of the work should be mailed to the following address:

Permissions Department
Sleepy Hollow Publishing
10424 Eastborne Ave
Los Angeles, CA 90024

Contact Information:
Pegi Burdick
Pegi@thefinancialwhisperer.com
ISBN 978-0-9853945-0-9

Disclaimer: The names, certain details and descriptions have been changed to protect the privacy of those I have spoken with and observed over the years. This book reflects my opinions, insights and conclusions.

The author and publisher disclaim any responsibility for loss, liability, or interpretation by the reader.

Dedication

This book is dedicated to Sophie Biddle, who taught me what it means to feel safe. She showed me that love is the most powerful four-letter word in any language. She demonstrated to me that one can control an elephant with a feather, and that kindness and softness can be the order of the day. Her tireless patience to read and re-read everything, every change, at least six times, gets her the Nobel Prize for being stalwart.

Acknowledgements

Where I am today is a direct result of meeting Dr. Ditta Oliker, my former therapist and now friend. I met her at my intersection of pain and hope 23 years ago. She gave me permission to be myself and to lead a life of empowerment and choice, teaching me that what happened to me as a young child was not my fault. She proved to me that when we are not living an authentic life, we feel powerless and disconnected. To survive our childhood we create an alternative persona, which is the premise of this book.

This book could not be now in your hands without my brother Josh's support and belief in this project. He also is a real life example of how two children from the same pathology can repair and heal their adult lives, even if it takes 60 years, proving it's never too late to love.

I had great people contribute to this project:

Amy Swift created the title and withstood my stubbornness about my thinking that I had the more accurate title.

Heidi Baer always asked questions that made me think and be accountable to my inner voice, even when it was silent.

Adryan Russ, whose patience with editing kept me calm and believing that I had something of value to even write about.

Amy Rachlin designed the cover and ignored my suggestions to have nine font styles, always citing: "It's just not good design."

Bridget Stout coordinated all the details and taught me to let the pros do their thing, even if it felt counter-intuitive.

Shirley Parker helped get me get unstuck a year ago to re-write what I had written four years ago. She got me to stand still, which I am not good at, and to re-connect with myself to do it.

Susan Piver, whom I have given direct credit to in some passages but also unnamed in some concepts. Her wisdom and sage advice saved my sanity more times than I can count.

George P. Putnam for his laser sharp final editing that he did with grace and humor.

Table of Contents

Introduction i

Chapter 1:
Where Are You Now? 1
    Loneliness: The Thief of Your Authentic Self 4
    Isolation: The Roadblock to Intimacy 10
    Helplessness: The Nemesis of Emotional Competence .. 16
    Depression: Anger Turned Inward 20

Chapter 2:
What's Holding You Back? 27
    Fear: The Undefined Future 31
    Shame: The More You Hide It, The Deeper It Gets 38
    Anger: A Clue to Unmet Needs 46
    Abandonment: The Underlying Fear 53

Chapter 3:
Engagement of the Outside World 61
    Procrastination: Free Beer Tomorrow 63
    Manipulation: Masking the Truth 70
    Chaos: The Enemy of Logic 78
    Perfection: The Journey Without a Destination 82

Chapter 4:
Getting Control 91
    Boundaries: Protection for Our Individual Souls 92
    Compassion: A Sense of Forgiveness 99
    Commitment: A Contract for Future Action 104
    Permission: The Gift of Letting Go 113

Chapter 5:
The Ultimate Goal **119**
   Healing: The Compass of Feeling............................ 120
   Trust: A Leap of Faith 127
   Intimacy: The Club We All Want to Belong to 131
   Forgiving: The Handmaiden of Trust 136

Afterword 139
Some Notes About How I Got Here............................ 143
Suggested Readings.. 147

Introduction

This book is based upon my Financial Whisperer® coaching series. It explains how, when our needs do not get properly met as young children, we create a survival system to manage the road ahead. This process can start as soon as we exit the womb. As adults, we can change our lives by embracing "emotional literacy." We can heal our past and return to our birthright of empowerment.

Because the need to survive is a primal drive, our greatest fear is to be abandoned. As Daniel Goleman concludes in his book, *Social Intelligence: The New Science of Social Relationships*[1], "The more strongly connected we are with someone emotionally, the greater the mutual force." The bond between a mother and her infant is unique and imprinted forever. Those early days of being out of the womb are precious for a child's sense of trust, as they are with every species.

---

[1] Goleman, Daniel. *Social Intelligence: The New Science of Social Relationships*. New York, NY: Bantam Dell, 2006.

It is that fear of abandonment that distorts our reality, holding us prisoner until we heal and let go — which we *can* learn to do. Most of us have already been abandoned once and are spending a lifetime trying to prevent it from happening again. In Brené Brown's book, *The Gifts of Imperfection*[2], she describes the word "belonging" as the innate need we all possess to be part of something larger, but the primal experience of truly belonging is for us to be seen authentically. To be accepted and valued as imperfect is the ultimate joy of intimacy and feeling safe.

In order to survive our childhood, we create a system that is all about reading signals and then making choices to support that system even when it really does not serve us well. I call this:

"Your Life On Two Tracks."

The two tracks represent you as an authentic person (how you *really* feel) and you as an adapted persona, that "other" you who you created in order to maintain your personal survival system.

---

[2] Brown, Brené. *The Gifts of Imperfection: Let Go of Who You Think You're Supposed to Be and Embrace Who You Are.* Center City, MN: Hazelden, 2010.

Introduction

These tracks are parallel; as one goes left, the other follows seamlessly without protest, until now. The "now" in your life is that maybe you suffer from bouts of depression, expressions of self-loathing, a constant sense of hopelessness and rage, feelings of isolation and the fear that you will never be happy, never be loved. And, you want your power back — you want to own your own life and have joy, finally.

In her book, *Hide and Seek*[3], Dr. Ditta Oliker uses Darwin's theory of survival as her basic premise, citing: "...what is true in the physical world is also true of the psychological world. Grasp the meaning of Darwin's concept of survival and you begin to understand the meaning and power of a psychological survival system." On your journey of gaining self-awareness, there will be many times that your life will feel like an emotional life-and-death battle. Just as an animal will struggle to stay alive when confronted by an enemy, your emotional and psychological sides will battle against their monsters.

---

[3] Oliker, Dr. Ditta M. *Hide and Seek: Reclaiming Childhood's Lost Potential.* Charleston, SC: BookSurge Publishing, 2010.

These dual tracks are the reason you can appear one way but actually be very different inside. This survival system, your second-track adapted persona, has outlived its purpose; you are no longer five years old and can now function with total autonomy. These old needs do not actually exist anymore, except in your head. How you move through the world versus how you feel should be consistent; it's when the two conflict that we shut down and sabotage ourselves. This is where we make poor financial choices, harm our bodies, and rationalize our negative behavior.

But, take heart, that intersection of conflict actually is the starting place to heal.

This book is organized into five chapters, each dealing with a different part of your personality, disposition and behavior. Each chapter takes words you already know and gives you a different perspective on how to use those words to best describe how you feel. Your feelings are your unique identity.

Take the example of the word *intimacy*. To most, it's about sex. What you will learn in this book is that intimacy is also about your soul, your innermost visceral feelings and how intimacy becomes part of your personal goal on your journey of healing. What you will learn in this

Introduction

book is that in order to connect with someone else, you must connect with yourself first, and how to do that now, as an adult.

Just like your life today, this book is full of metaphors and symbols. The financial issues you struggle with today are not really only about dollars and cents, they are about deeper, older issues you have carried with you since your youth.

> ***The journey of healing starts with choice: Walk into the light. You are the one you have been waiting for.*[4]**

---

[4] *Daily Om*, newsletter, 12/2/2007.

CHAPTER 1
WHERE ARE YOU NOW?

This wagon wheel, with its splintered hub, represents your life as it is today. Here's how. Everything in your life is interrelated; when the core of who you are is cracked, it wobbles and feels out of control. Regaining control is the journey of self-discovery, the journey of ownership.

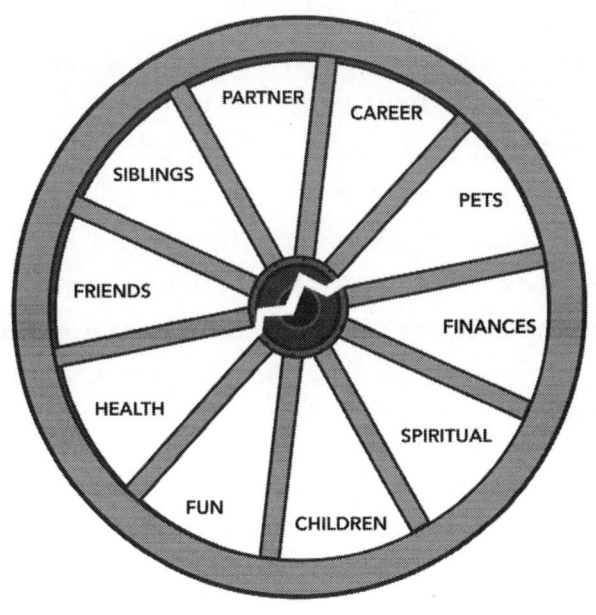

It's NEVER About The Money... Even When It Is

When a client came to me because she believed she was having financial problems, she soon discovered it was not her lack of money that was causing her grief. The real source of pain was her profound sense of not feeling wanted. Her parents had cared for her physical needs when she was a child, but emotionally had left her on her own. Her deeply felt sense of not being *attached* to anything or anyone led her to attempt to fill the void with shopping.

While it was her ongoing shopping that was getting her into financial difficulty, it was her inability to recognize what was causing her to shop that was doing her in.

Now she has been learning how to gain self-awareness and how to heal wounds from her childhood that have controlled her adult life. She is one of the reasons I've written this book. I know many of you out there have financial issues and you've been traveling old, familiar roads, not finding the answers you need. The right path is waiting for you if you're willing to take the journey with me.

Where Are You Now?

> *"Two roads diverged in a wood, and I,*
> *I took the one less traveled by,*
> *And that has made all the difference."*
>   **Robert Frost**
>   **The Road Not Taken**

Are you familiar with this poem? Most of us do not take the road that makes the difference, but maybe this time you can. Let's begin with your state of being. Where are you now? How are you feeling? Feelings are the basis of a person's identity. How you manage your feelings in the moment speaks volumes about your sense of self-worth and the self-worth of that inner child who lives inside us all.

Beginning with your life, as it feels right now, let's examine when you feel lonely, your bouts of isolation, heavy feelings of helplessness and battles with depression. They are all interrelated spokes in the wheel of your life that strongly affect your balance.

LONELINESS:
THE THIEF OF YOUR AUTHENTIC SELF

I once asked a client how she would define loneliness. Her struggle to find the right words demonstrated her experience with it. She gave me some examples of when she was lonely, but she could not pinpoint the common factor among them.

I asked her, "Is it that nobody *gets* you?"

Her eyes lit up with acknowledgement.

"Yes!" she exclaimed. And then she started to cry softly because the reservoir of pain she had been carrying her entire 48 years had been identified. The mere fact that someone could identify that deep well in her psyche was in itself a form of being *gotten*.

Feeling as if no one *gets* you is debilitating. It leaves you unable to share yourself. No matter what you do or say, no one truly understands you. In that moment, you feel totally alone. After a series of such encounters, the loneliness intensifies. The connection to another human being is what would make you feel whole, and the possibility of such an event becomes the biggest seducer of them all.

This desperation to feel connected drives us to form unions we normally would reject. It pulls us into circumstances that often don't resonate with our authentic self. If no one truly heard you as a child, your assumption growing up is that nobody will ever see you for who you really are.

That was something you may have learned as a child that was true then and isn't true now — but you still believe it. The question is: Why do you still need to believe it?

Having spent your entire life on an adapted track in order to survive has its price. People who refuse to acknowledge their loneliness sometimes get confused because they may spend all day around others but still feel lonely. Continuing to deny feelings only increases the sense of isolation, which is the foundation of loneliness. When we learn to use accurate ways to describe our feelings, we begin to shift.

Living your life on two tracks is going to make you feel that something is vaguely "wrong." Rooted in a childhood of disconnection, you always feel as if you are a fraud in some way.

> **When we live a fraudulent life, we don't have enough touchstones to connect with others, and with our inner selves.**

We do have fleeting small moments of joy, connectedness, hope and belonging. When we allow ourselves to be compromised in the hope that, this time, everything will be okay, and this relationship will last, we are giving away our power, setting ourselves up for disappointment. But again, the circus that came to town departs, and we are left with popped balloons, broken dreams, and discarded fantasies.

Dr. Sue Johnson, the Canadian author and therapist, describes primal attachment as "the human hunger to find a safe emotional connection."[5] That need then controls our choices, good or bad. We sometimes look back, as I personally have done, with jobs, ex-husbands, former friends and ask: "What was I thinking?" Were my needs so disguised that I could not clearly evaluate what was best for me? Apparently

---

[5] Johnson, Dr. Sue. *Hold Me Tight: Seven Conversations for a Lifetime of Love.* New York, NY: Little, Brown & Company, 2008.

so, which accounts for why I ended up with huge debts in my 50s. Something else was driving my bus; something else had control over me.

We are social animals needing love in order to feel a sense of value and purpose. Anything other than that plays itself out in the material world in a variety of ways, including how we handle money. It becomes a statement about our inner world. We all have friends who shop, eat or drink too much or constantly pick up the dinner check for the whole group in order to deny their feelings of loneliness.

The emptiness we feel in the pit of our stomachs is unbearable. As we begin to live a more authentic life, the emptiness, the overindulging, the feelings of loneliness, and other painful emotions shrink and we feel freer and freer.

JESSICA

Jessica had been living a two-track life. As she began to talk about her childhood, I saw why she was having money issues. Her parents made it abundantly clear to her, when she was very little, that she was an unexpected birth — not wanted, only tolerated. She was an inconvenience.

Her parents went through all the traditional steps of caring for her physical needs, but they never had time for her. They would watch TV, but have no time to help her with her homework or Girl Scouts. They avoided activities that required their 100% attention. As a result, Jessica became an avid reader. She grew up lonely because her parents did not reach out to her and create the bonds necessary for her to feel whole.

Jessica does not have to stay that way for the rest of her life. Gaining self-awareness helps give her the power to choose to heal, starting right now. As an adult, she can begin to do things for herself that her mother should have done. Her mother should have given Jessica her undivided attention, or been 100% present when she noticed Jessica drifting. Parents need to give children their presence and patience.

As Susan Piver says, "Attention is the most basic form of love."[6] Now Jessica can give her inner child the attention her mother failed to give.

---

[6] Piver, Susan. *How Not to Be Afraid of Your Own Life: Opening Your Heart to Confidence, Intimacy and Joy.* New York, NY: St. Martin's Press, 2006.

How Does Loneliness Connect to Money?

Why did Jessica pick finances to express her pain? In society, one's value, unfortunately, is often defined by how much money we have, how much we make, and how much we spend. For someone feeling valueless, this is a perfect dynamic to express pain and worthlessness. Having money, or the result of how we manage it, is very external, very visible. Earning money often is the reflection of performance; the harder or smarter you work, the more money you make.

But many of us got a different message early on: "Don't compete, don't step out of the shadows into the light, for you will steal glory and love from your siblings. There is only *one* reward and it will go only to him or her — not you. Only one can win; there is no second place in this race."

So we shut down, divert our real feelings, and in doing so, once again support our adapted, unauthentic-self track.

It's time to take the road not taken — to decide if you will seek love and control. What is your Achilles heel? What are your predominant, innate skills? What do you love about yourself? What gives you pleasure? Identify them and pop them into your tool belt. You're going to need them on this new journey.

Isolation:
The Roadblock to Intimacy

Isolation is a distancing tool — retreating into our own emotional space. It's about defending ourselves by creating a space between "us" and "them." Us is our inner four-year-old. Them includes everyone in the outside world along with factors a four-year-old cannot predetermine. It's a common trap that young children create when there aren't enough "connectors" to keep them engaged.

As we get older, that tool stays with us. We can be 15 or 95 years old and still use isolation as a way to express our fears. It is, in part, a statement of a lack of intimacy with one's self.

Isolation starts in a subtle way, sometimes appearing as irritability or listlessness, revealing no effect, being flat in our demeanor, forgetful, or unresponsive. All of this can be easily disguised in a highly functioning person who gives the appearance of being present, or who may act grandiose or arrogant, but emotionally has "left the building."

When someone is feeling isolated, it is not the time to ask that person for a favor; anything you ask will be met with resentment and bare effort. Often when people are in retreat mode, they become couch potatoes and zone out by watching videos, eating — dulling their brains in some way. Or, they are out there, "dancing as fast as they can." Either way, they are emotionally lost — a dinghy at sea, bobbing up and down, no tether to connect to the shore. Or, they may engage in an activity they know will sabotage themselves; they will not be present, in the moment, authentic. Emotionally, they will be on the sidelines as observers. They will offer seemingly confusing signals.

> *Isolation is really a cry for help. No one can hear the cry, because the person is in a glass prison.*

Why does the child, now an adult, choose isolation as a hiding place? Based on conversations with people over the last five years, I have seen that the common thread always appears to be fear — the fear of expressing needs. For some of us, having needs feels shameful.

What do children do when their needs are constantly marginalized, when they are rejected for complaining that no one ever listens, and as they get older, experience shame for needing something? They retreat. Those children will lack an internal sense of competence and may appear withdrawn, shy, and avoid contact — the very thing they need to bring their dinghy home.

When we are in our "cave" moments, which can last for days, sometimes the simplest connection can shift our perceptions and break our self-imposed solitude. Helping someone do something, which could be met with the most sincere gratitude, makes us feel visible, useful, appreciated. Suddenly, we do exist, we do matter, and we are lovable.

Children need, early on, to feel competent and capable so, as they get older, their ability to trust their own instincts gets cemented and they are able to stay in the present moment.

How does a mother help her child build self-sufficiency? Let's say the child is five, content to be by himself, involved in an activity, a craft, reading, or looking at bugs on the ground. The activity challenges him to be engaged with himself, and he enjoys that interaction with his imagination. Children are naturally curious and clever.

Those magical moments are undisguised and unrehearsed and allow a young child to be carefree and totally self-absorbed. He is innocent and everything in front of him is new, whether it's an infant discovering his belly button or a child trying to glue bread together to make a sandwich for the dog.

These moments are critical to a child's sense of confidence, which is built upon self-esteem. If a child has a mother who constantly interrupts those moments, made worse by the mother trying to get her own needs met, the child never experiences the sense of accomplishment and pride. This child needs to be acknowledged — and rewarded.

Confirming a child's self-esteem is the mother's task at hand, which means the child's natural state of trusting instincts and trusting himself starts to build. In the absence of that kind of mother, father, siblings, aunts or other people to support them in this way, to create their backup system, the child doesn't feel safe. That's where the Isolation Monster starts to creep in.

> **When there is a real lack of stability, instead of feeling excited about the unknown, a child feels fear.**

That fear then becomes the controlling device that pulls a person into isolation. It goes on for a lifetime if one does not connect the dots.

THE DISCOUNT SHOPPER

A woman in a workshop of mine would spend her money at many discount stores, never really paying attention to what she was buying. Those items would end up in her garage sale or be given away months down the road.

She was buying these things at, let's say, the 99 Cents store, and they had no value for her. The things she really wanted she would not buy because she didn't think she deserved them. She went ahead and spent nickels and dimes on smaller things, which never satisfied her. As we discovered, she had no intimacy with her husband, children or family members. Her isolation was a result of her lack of self-worth.

We have funny ways of expressing our isolation. There isn't always a clear cause and effect. It controls us, but it hides underneath other behaviors.

In talking recently with a client struggling with her bouts of depression that sit atop isolation, I asked her to think about being on two shores — "here," where you are right now, and "there," where you really want to be, if it was safe.

"You need a bridge," I said, which is an activity that connects you to your authentic self. "So, let's define something you love and use it now as the bridge."

I explained that when you do something you love, you connect the parts of yourself that give you a sense of wholeness. Love is about wholeness.

She said that she loves to cook but sometimes wants to take a nap when she thinks about it. So, I told her that was self-sabotage holding her back. My antidote was to get busy doing something else, like cleaning the grout of her kitchen tile with a toothbrush. Then, as she is scrubbing, she could think about the smells of the ragu she could be making. Then making the decision between garlic bread and no garlic bread, she would discover that she would be making the shopping list in her head. After finishing the grout (or not), she would get to the store and start cooking. As a result of this process, the feeling of isolation would disappear.

This tool is all part of re-connecting with the things in your life that define who you are. Writing this book has been the bridge that has kept me grounded during a challenging time.

What will you choose as your bridge?

HELPLESSNESS:
THE NEMESIS OF EMOTIONAL COMPETENCE

Acting helpless is a great way to avoid seeing one's potential. I have seen this often with adults who are last born, or twins; an older sibling will "take care" of the situation; one of the twins is more outgoing and assertive.

If a parent is not watchful, that "take care" action will rob the other child of opportunities to experience himself as capable. Even small activities, such as tying shoelaces, bringing groceries into the house, teaching the dog to sit, writing checks to pay the bills (great exercise for a nine-year-old), keeping one's room tidy, all help a young child experience himself as capable and responsible.

As children get older, the tasks become more sophisticated, and need to be appreciated by all. A simple "thank you" goes a long way to not feeling taken for granted.

> ***How many kids grow up in a house where they feel invisible, where no one expects anything from them, and no one acknowledges they exist — until they get into trouble?***

Helplessness is sometimes a passive-aggressive statement used to express anger or a misplaced sense of entitlement. Sometimes it sits beneath the victim lament: "Why can't I have (fill in the blank)?"

LUANNE

Luanne complained that she had disappointing friends who never kept tennis dates, showed up late for tee times at the golf course, or did not return telephone calls in a timely manner. She always ended up feeling she did not matter.

So, I asked, "Why do you associate with people who don't reflect your values?" Clearly, she did not feel worthy. Although, with some self-awareness, she could make other choices, she chose to stay in the darkness, which reflected her upbringing — her comfort zone. It's easier to complain than to try to fix a situation. She continuously created situations that left her feeling "less than," instead of whole and nurtured.

Feeling competent is a one-way street; once you allow yourself to move forward on your own power, you can't go back to the stagnation of helplessness.

> ***It's a slow process. You need to be patient and compassionate with yourself. Seeing yourself from a new perspective takes getting used to.***

This explains why so many lottery winners end up in bankruptcy, why people yo-yo diet and can never seem to make the weight loss permanent, and why staying sober is a full-time job.

What do people gain from acting helpless? Helplessness reinforces the false sense of comfort that comes from thinking that if you stay in the shadows, you have succeeded in fooling the monsters in the closet to not abandon you.

Yet, the day comes when you will start to feel anger, shame, embarrassment and self-consciousness — that the "party bus" is moving on without you, and you will be left behind. Same debt, same weight, same alcohol, same sense of emptiness; your life feels as if someone else has been living it.

"Who is that person?" you will ask. It's not someone you respect. It's not someone you want to take to the party with you if you were to be invited. Feeling helpless is being a victim. It makes you feel powerless.

Where Are You Now?

How Does Helplessness Connect to Money?

Luanne's constant job changing reflected her posture as the victim; never doing what gave her life meaning, always living paycheck to paycheck, she never saw her life in "the big picture." Her finances were scattered and she never wanted to really see what was going on.

In spending more time connecting her current behavior to old childhood assumptions, she started to exercise more control, take back her power and protest less that things were not her fault.

What are you protesting today that's not your fault?

Depression:
Anger Turned Inward

Depression is the ultimate "drug" for removal from the moment. It takes us out of the line of fire by making us act emotionally dead and lifeless. We become a spectator.

It is a subtle form of manipulation — being physically present and emotionally absent. It can even invite a strong negative response from those around the depressed person. One hears such comments as, "Time to get going!" "Move on." "Snap out of it!" "Stop acting so grumpy." Or, "Slow down! Why can't you make time for (fill in the blank)?"

The common definition of depression is anger turned inward. Why do we use it? Where does the anger come from, and how do we change that way of expressing ourselves?

There are many ways one can express depression, but the underlying consistent root is separating one from one's authentic self, which, in many cases, is due to acute pain and fear — all statements of a misperceived lack of power.

People have choices in which mode they show up — which costume fits their need to stay in the shadows. Some people pick weight, others choose debt, drugs or depression — and the list gets longer. Some withdraw and appear lifeless, helpless and without effect. They cannot get out of bed or off the sofa; they feel powerless and trapped. Or they can be overly busy, always in motion. They are angry but cannot identify their anger. Depression is a defense mechanism. Addiction is a form of depression.

> **When we use a secondary form of expression — such as debt, food, alcohol, misspending, or chaos — we create a smokescreen that takes on its own life. It's a form of denial that distracts the outside world. Whatever form of expression we choose can create shame, which separates us from our authentic self.**

Accepting the fact that anger sits underneath depression, it is important to understand where the anger comes from. Not getting our needs met as very young children initiates the assumption that we are not worthy of love.

Where our lives go from that very early message is the explanation for our current negative behaviors. Depression is a fear-based expression — fear of being seen for how we *really* feel, who we *really* are. We were warned early on in our childhoods that we needed to conform in order to survive. As a result, we isolated ourselves in order to protect our true feelings — our identities.

Alice Miller writes, in *The Drama of the Gifted Child*,[7] "...the true opposite of depression is neither gaiety nor absence of pain, but vitality — the freedom to experience spontaneous feelings, which is crucially important for us if we want to live without depression and addiction."

In medical journals, articles by psychologists abound with debates as to whether depression is a chemical or environmental issue. There is no question that certain drugs will alter one's mood, but in some cases drugs will disguise the underlying source and make managing the moment ahead easier. One out of five Americans takes some sort of medication to manage stress, to regulate moods, to cope better.

We are a society that does what is easy — taking a diet pill is easier than dealing with the underlying issues of *why* we eat out of control;

---

[7] Miller, Alice. *The Drama of the Gifted Child: The Search for the True Self.* New York, NY: Basic Books, 1997.

taking a sleeping pill is easier than taking the time to understand our adrenal system and hormones; taking a mood elevator in some cases just pushes away dealing with the intense inner pain that needs to be acknowledged.

> ***The key to prevent depression is to own your power by building self-awareness.***

When we are depressed, fear and anger own us. As adults, we actually have choices that we lacked as children.

I have had many clients who struggle with isolation, which is fueled by shame, which in turn, looks like depression. Many of them had the same retreat mode: stay in bed, on the sofa. Work longer office hours. Do more pushups, run more errands. They do anything and everything to avoid *feeling* the underlying issue.

VANESSA

Vanessa was the oldest of two children and the only girl. She was an image consultant working with Fortune 500 companies, training incoming staff on their appearances, appropriate dress, and behavior conducive to a professional atmosphere.

No one would ever guess that her personal behavior at home lacked polish and boundaries. For her, working was her only real connection with the outside world. She was a functioning depressed person; her relationship with her brother suffered constant friction — her parents continued to infantilize him through adulthood. This behavior on their part continued siphoning off attention that she had needed as a child and, as an adult, would never experience. Her parents' subtle message to her was: "Your brother's needs are more important than yours."

Every session always came back to her suppressed anger; how it got displayed in subtle actions during her day, and not-so-subtle behaviors when she left her office. Our constant tying of her feelings of depression to her anger helped her identify her trigger-points so she could manage the moment better.

By learning a new vocabulary, she developed tools to identify what was actually going on in the moment, thereby giving her the power to choose a behavior that would serve her best.

How Does Depression Connect to Money?

Vanessa's primary financial issue was careless spending, but it did not go over the edge. She just felt nothing, deadness. No joy in a new item, always wearing the same basic style day after day, never allowing herself to experience something new. She never felt connected to what she was purchasing, as if it would be a statement of lack of control. Basically, she simply made herself numb.

Her challenge, as it is for us all, was to live in the present moment, completely. She had to give herself permission to *feel* that whatever was going on was legitimate for her and then choose how to react.

Her journey to become more present started with creating plans and keeping commitments to herself. It was the beginning of her healing. She is finally being heard now as an adult and is able to express her needs without fear of recrimination, which has reduced isolation and shame.

She is on her way. How about you? Have you strapped on your tool belt and laced up your hiking boots?

Chapter 2:
What's Holding You Back?

The pyramids on the next page represent feelings that cause loneliness, isolation, helplessness and depression. The point at the top is the trigger. When one gets disconnected, that emotion is the first that's visible. But it's actually masking a feeling underneath. As you dig further down, you hit another layer of emotion that's being covered over; dig more and you come to yet another emotion. Dig as you will as you gain self-awareness, and when you reach the bottom you will find that fear we all have — the fear of abandonment. Everyone has a way of moving through the world, some of us lead with suppressed anger, some with deadness, others with sadness that can mask shame.

It's NEVER About The Money... Even When It Is

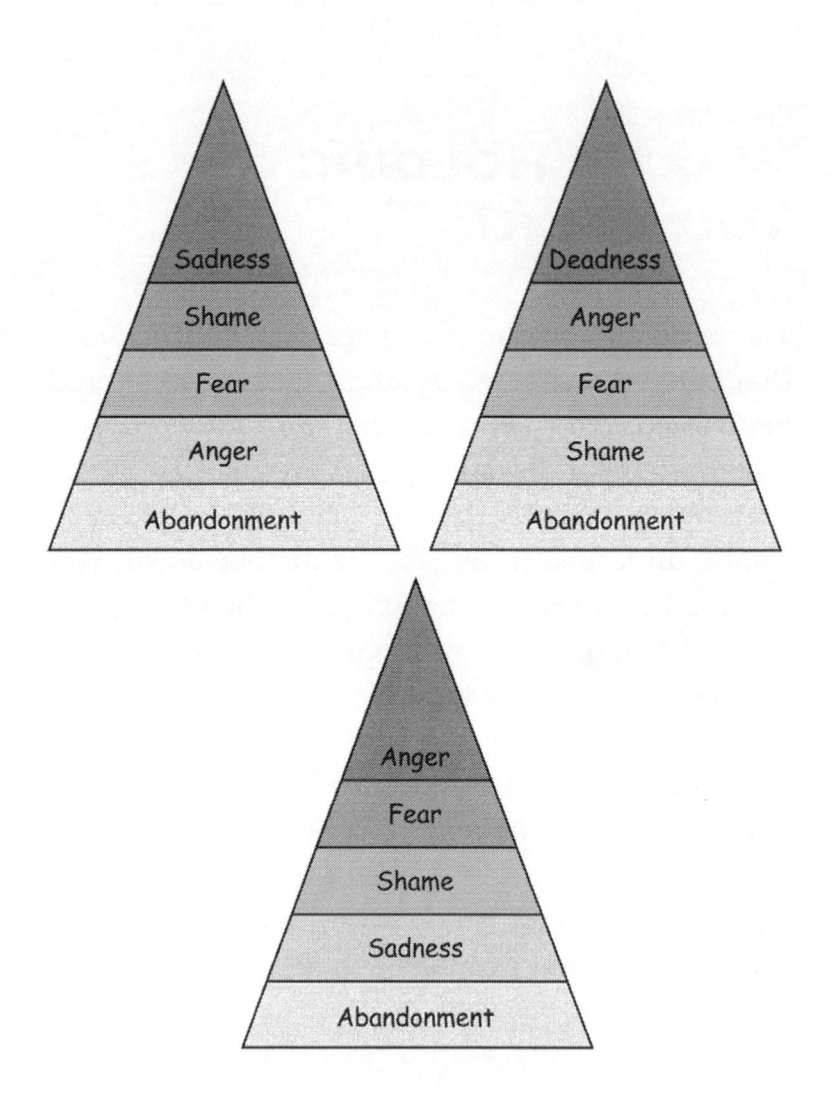

Pyramid 1
- Sadness
- Shame
- Fear
- Anger
- Abandonment

Pyramid 2
- Deadness
- Anger
- Fear
- Shame
- Abandonment

Pyramid 3
- Anger
- Fear
- Shame
- Sadness
- Abandonment

What's Holding You Back?

Do you feel that something is standing in the way of having joy in your life? What is it? Can you take a guess? We all have moments when we sabotage ourselves, but, busy as we are, we don't always take the time to look at why we do it. Are you ready to see how and why you do it? It's simply a matter of examining a few factors — perhaps you have a fear of abandonment, suppressed anger you've been holding on to for a long time, and even some underlying shame. Once you begin to take a look at these possibilities, you become open to discovering what steps you can take to reverse them. Burying fear and anger does nothing to help us. Looking at them while acknowledging what they do to us does.

The reality is that so many of our behaviors today, even if we are 45 years old, are rooted in early childhood experiences that we're still reacting to as if we are five years old. Even though those perceptions were cemented a long time ago, they live on, in full color, as if they were happening today.

This is true of lots of things in life — our feelings, for example. Feeling shame affects our feelings of anger. When we act in fearful ways, our actions might come across as impatience. When we resist intimacy, it's a sign that we are not feeling a sense of trust. All of these emotions have equal energies; they all rub up against each other. Let's take a look at the emotion that tends to trigger all the others and surrounds us when we're feeling held back.

FEAR:
THE UNDEFINED FUTURE

The dictionary defines fear as the anticipation of danger. I suppose that's true. But if we look at fear compassionately, as something that needs attention, it's actually a tool, a clue. It gives us a window into our youth — a way to view how we saw the world when we were three, four or five years old.

Where does fear come from? In Susan Piver's book, *How Not to Be Afraid of Your Own Life*, she pinpoints how it begins in infancy, the result of feeling that our need for warmth, closeness and acceptance is being rejected. When babies cry, those are some of the things they want and often don't get.

Fear is the opposite of trust. The level of discomfort we can experience from fear can be so extreme that our bodies change temperature, our stomachs get acidy, our palms sweat, our breathing changes, we can grow passive, totally withdraw into our own world, go lifeless, or become aggressive.

When we are experiencing fear, often we'll react with decisions we later regret. Have you done that? I have. Who or what really has control in those fearful moments? Your authentic self? Definitely not. Your adapted persona? More likely. In fearful moments and situations, we allow our adapted track in our life to decide what the next ten minutes or the next day will be for us. Why do we do that? It's a bit like traveling outside our bodies, feeling the need to be someone we aren't. Then, when the fear passes, we smack ourselves on the forehead and ask, "What was I thinking?" We beat ourselves up for being "wrong" when all we were trying to do was protect ourselves.

> ***Who are we really afraid of?***
> ***What are we really afraid of?***

BARBARA

Talking with Barbara in our first session revealed that her fear of other women was so paralyzing, she would get a painful stomachache when she knew she had to go to a PTA meeting.

When she would see other mothers, Barbara felt inadequate, which to the outside world would be astounding, because she is a well-known fashion model who has graced the pages of *Vogue*, *Harper's* and *People* magazines. Who would ever think she had a problem with other women? She expressed herself by remaining slightly aloof, seeming snooty at times. She always assumed women were talking about her and criticizing her behind her back. Who would ever guess she was dying inside to be accepted and liked?

Barbara's mother died when she was eight years old. In subsequent sessions, we uncovered that days prior to her mother's death from a stroke, she had heard her parents talking to the school about her poor grades, and heard her mother ask the teacher if it was possible that Barbara was retarded.

Barbara knew what retarded meant; she felt embarrassed, ashamed and angry with her mother. She had so much anger that she wished her mother would die. A week later, her mother did die.

Barbara believed she had killed her mother. No one in her house would talk about her mother's passing; she had gone to a friend's for a sleepover, her mother had helped her pack her little suitcase, she came home the next morning and her mother was gone. Her father, uncles and aunts were silent. Barbara was confused, frightened, and there was no one to talk to. She felt responsible, ashamed, terrified and very alone.

A week later, when she returned to school after the funeral, she could see the other girls whispering to each other. She assumed they were telling each other that Barbara had killed her mother.

This is a classic example of wrongly assuming what one sees. Fear can distort reality and imprint an assumption that gets rooted in that fear. The girls were probably talking about her dress, her sadness, and that they too were frightened. But Barbara's guilt over wishing for her mother's death distorted everything she experienced. As we talked about her fears of the other "scary moms," as she called them, other feelings surfaced: shame, for example.

As soon as we exposed this major piece of hidden emotion in Barbara's past and she began to understand how she had been distorting the past in order to hold on to the shame, which was part of her identity, her present experiences shifted. From that day forth, she never gave the "scary PTA moms" another thought.

Fear can feel like a vapor — it feels cold to some, hot to others. It envelops us in mystery that can make us crazy about the future. Life can get complicated because we *can* love and feel fear at the same time. This becomes most evident with family members; we can love our siblings on one level, yet be afraid of them on another.

When fear takes us over, we get busy trying to find solutions to make it disappear. But it doesn't. There's a good reason for that. Trying to hide it just makes it sit inside and stew. The most effective way to manage fear is to be still — and just let it *be*. Creating a relationship with fear, allowing it to wash over our bodies and just sit with it, like an old friend, helps us to be open and receptive.

> ***The right solution comes naturally when you stay calm and open. Awareness and compassion will bring an answer that's true to who you are.***

Again, from Susan Piver's book, breathing deeply and looking right at your fear, for as many seconds as long as it appears to be there, is the best way to make it less scary. If your mind is busy either looking for a solution or denying it, neither will help you, and nothing will happen. Befriending the fear and giving it a seat on the bus next to you will give you peace, grounding, and perspective and have you feeling powerful.

When we ignore our feelings, we abandon ourselves. It's an act of attempting to escape from one's self, which is the exact opposite of what we need to do. It duplicates exactly what was done to us when we were small. If you knew you were continuing to abandon yourself, you wouldn't do it anymore, would you? Children are not born fearful. Fearful parents pass their fears onto their children, so fear is a learned behavior. That's why we need to look at those feelings, let them exist, be open to them — so we can learn why they are there, and move forward.

How Does Fear Connect to Money?

A lack of self-worth can readily be tied to money. Money stands for value in a certain context; so money can become an external mirror of our internal value. We create our belief of how much we should be paid based on our own perception of our self-worth, which, if distorted by a sense of inadequacy and fear, sets a low price for ourselves. As a result, the impulse is to keep a low profile, stay below the radar, and earn less.

At the other extreme, of course, is an inflated sense of self-worth, demanding money disproportionate to the task or our value. Where do you fit in this model? Do you think you under-estimate your self-worth or overestimate it?

Shame:
The More You Hide It, The Deeper It Gets

Shame is huge. Quoting psychologist Michael Lewis, medical correspondent Holly VanScoy calls it "the quintessential emotion."[8] Says Donald I. Nathanson, M.D., "All extravagant behaviors are reactions to it."

Shame is a learned response resulting from adult comments and behaviors designed to control a child's behavior. It's often generational, passed down from parent to child, and then to the child's child. As a controlling device that meets the dysfunctional needs of a parent, it will reappear in negative behaviors as the child grows up.

It can take a lifetime of healing to finally sooth the wounds of shame. As Brené Brown wrote in her book, *I Thought It Was Just Me*,[9] "The more one hides their shame, the deeper it gets."

It is the primary caretaker's responsibility to give the newborn child a sense of value, joy and pleasure, which is the beginning foundation of self-

---

[8] http://soulselfhelp.on.ca/quintessentialemotion.html
[9] Brown, Brené. *I Thought It Was Just Me (but it isn't): Telling the Truth About Perfectionism, Inadequacy and Power.* New York, NY: Gotham Books, 2007.

worth. It is that caretaker's responsibility to protect that young child. It's the mother's responsibility to cement a sense of trust, which starts at birth. If that fails, the child experiences a disconnection, which slowly triggers adaptation to take form. Children are very intuitive, even as young as a week old.

Dr. Alen J. Salerian, Medical Director at Washington Psychiatric Center, notes that shame is a complex emotional response learned in early childhood development. "In many situations, it would be abnormal if we did not experience it,"[10] he says.

Most parents are emotional train wrecks themselves because they never got a "clean" start; *their* lives were shaped by *their* parents, and their environment is what fueled their assumptions.

> ***The double standards that most people live by, combined with their own survival system, create the nest that their own children ultimately grow up in. Children observe what adults and older siblings do and how***

---

[10] http://www.salerianbrain.com/?p=38

> **they do it. For them, this is a clue as to what is assumed to be acceptable behavior, or what is not.**

So, if our parents toss trash out the window of the car, we're likely to do the same. If they yell and scream, we will too. But, when they tell us not to smoke, curse or be disrespectful, and yet they do all those things, we get confused over the double standard. Being consistent is a major socializing tool. It teaches a child about trust — or becomes a warning *not* to trust. It teaches predictability.

Our caregivers are supposed to put our needs first. Often they attach criticism to our wanting, suddenly making that wanting "bad." Therefore, we are "bad" for wanting it. It's the *way* they say no that either diminishes or confirms us. The consistency of ridicule, abuse, and humiliation eats away at a child's self-esteem, pushing the child into becoming hypersensitive.

> **As Dr. Marilyn Sorensen puts it, "...shame is the feeling of being something wrong."[11]**

---

[11] http://psychcentral.com/lib/2006/shame-the-quintessential-emotion/all/1/

When adults are consistent in their reproaches, *that* feeling gets cemented. As we get older, we feel shame when those feelings are activated. In those nanoseconds, we are transported back to when we were five and felt uncomfortable because we expressed a need and were criticized for the desire. That trip back in time takes seconds. With one phrase, we are back there, and suffering those feelings again. Does this sound familiar?

Because shame is generational, parents who carry it around with them cannot focus on their child's needs because they are too busy trying to get their own needs met. Often that shame blossoms into contempt for one's self, motivating choices that are self-destructive, staying in a toxic relationship, treating one's self with no respect, focusing on what we don't have, and refusing to believe that we can change the future.

HOW DO SHAME AND MONEY CONNECT?

Women have a lot of shame surrounding money. We learn it from a dynamic in our household, which is about power and who has it. The asking for money, the need for it, and the desire to make a statement in a society that was created by men send women into deep conflict. Women traditionally were not the breadwinners; they were the hearth tenders, the quilt makers, and the nest makers. Men were out fighting wars, foraging for food, finding ways to support and protect their families. So, it's only very recently — in the last 70 years — that women have stepped forward to claim financial entitlements.

In my generation, there was one breadwinner: Dad. He held the power and the money. It's no wonder that women have so many issues surrounding money. We were taught to marry a rich guy, have children and live happily ever after. This is so engrained in us that it's almost part of our DNA.

When women have self-esteem issues, asking for money is demeaning. Asking for any kind of help can be humiliating. Letting the outside world know that you have needs can feel shameful. Women often shut down and suffer silently, not realizing that the woman in the house next door is feeling exactly the same way. The isolation builds. Fear, the underlying emotion that seems to trigger all others, takes over — and this time it's the fear of falling down financially and not being able to get back up. Being broke and alone is a woman's greatest fear.

What's Holding You Back?

What sets shame apart is the denial that comes with it. Often when I start a conversation about how shame shows up, a client will deny that she feels shame, not realizing how many of us feel shame about the most basic experiences. When have you felt shame? It could have been something subtle and fleeting, but it's there.

Shame is about who you are intrinsically. It's not guilt, but sometimes gets confused with it. It's not embarrassment, but can feel like it until one connects the right vocabulary to the correct feeling.

Remember Barbara, who had a paralyzing fear of other women? When we talked, another piece of her fear emerged, which was the profound sense of shame she walked around with, which could get ignited by her husband's moodiness. Her shame, at least in part, came from spankings she had been given with a hairbrush by a nanny.

Her mother was bedridden and her father worked long hours. Barbara's needs for her mother kept getting criticized; and worse, she was beaten for asking to be held, asking to be nurtured. As a result, as an adult, she rarely asks for help and tries to do everything on her own. She cringes over the necessity to ask for assistance and will go to great lengths to avoid that shameful moment. Isn't it amazing how this has stuck with her all these years, even though she's long been an adult?

Helping Barbara understand her feelings of shame allowed her to embrace the belief that if she could trust herself, the shame would disappear. Once she understood this, the trust started to build, and the shame began to dissipate.

Some Observations About Shame:

- Secrets support shame
- Secrets perpetuate a double-track life
- Shame is the opposite of spirituality
- Shame is the opposite of creativity
- Shame is the opposite of respect
- Shame won't allow trust in
- Shame is like a robe placed onto you; you are the innocent receiver
- Shame births insecurities, shyness, isolation and hidden anger

Letting go of your shame allows healing, breaks the vicious cycle, and gives you a second chance at true respect, trust and love.

The exercises I recommend start with keeping commitments to yourself, which enables you to gain self-respect. In that process, the doors that have held shame hidden slowly start to open.

> ***Compassion and softness help us***
> ***accept our self, so that we can get on***
> ***the road to releasing shame.***
> ***The destination is intimacy.***
> ***Did you find your canteen yet?***
> ***Grab on to your pith helmet.***

Anger: A Clue to Unmet Needs

Anger is commonly defined as strong displeasure. But, like many other negative emotions, it can serve as an opportunity to learn more about ourselves, to experience, for example, early childhood circumstances whose details, long forgotten, are still alive — and figure out what our anger is about. While our childhood is long gone, the *feelings* from that time are not only still there, but are cemented — hardened over time, but easily cracked if we simply allow ourselves to be open to them.

Anger shows up as a result of a boundary breached, or not getting our needs met. It can be a power struggle between two entities whose needs are conflicting. These unmet needs, strange as it may seem, likely started at birth, at a time when, as infants, we are 100% dependent upon caregivers.

Elevated anger is the precursor of violence, which when unchecked can have dire consequences. It's sometimes a tinderbox of repressed and suppressed emotions that erupt with such force that everyone goes scurrying — or worse, people get trapped and abused by the explosive person. We've seen this happen when "nice" people suddenly explode and wind up killing others.

Anger can be expressed by coldness, silence or by being withdrawn. But the point to remember is that the way people express their anger is a learned behavior from infancy.

> ***How our caregivers reacted to our crying and fussing lays the groundwork for future expectations and assumptions about our own needs.***

While it is my belief that anger basically comes from unmet childhood needs, I have learned that, in order to understand something, one must sometimes look at the opposite experience to gain clarity and make deductions. So, whenever I meet contented and confident young people, I ask about their mothers and family dynamics. With amazing consistency, children whose needs were met appropriately end up being grounded adults, making decisions that support their true desires, and who behave in a consistently authentic manner. Adults who grew up with emotionally healthy parents can express themselves without fear of reprisal, and witness someone else's anger without personalizing it.

The manner in which infants' needs are met determines how and when their lives go off on another track. This time is critical to the future of a child; this turning point is the beginning of the infant's survival instincts kicking in and determining whether being authentic is being celebrated or confined. In other words, do I continue to be seen for who I really am (having needs) or shift and adapt to who they want me to be so they don't get angry with me? Does this ring true in your life? It certainly did in mine. It's all about survival.

Because surviving is the number-one drive in any species, the message the child adapts to is: if you mask your true feelings and change the way you appear, you will be taken care of and loved. Failure to do so will result in you being ignored, punished, shamed — thrown off the bus, so to speak. Being authentic becomes unacceptable. Why do people do this to one another? Because that's how they were brought up.

There have been scores of books and theories promoting different parenting methods that keep mothers dancing in the darkness of their insecurities.

> **What many fail to see and talk about is this: A mother's primary responsibility is to meet her infant's needs 100% in the early months and gradually shift as the infant becomes more autonomous.**
>
> **Those critical first 1-9 months that the infant is out of the womb is the time for bonding. This ensures the child's sense of trust and expectations.**

An infant needs to *feel* that his or her needs come first. Infants totally depend upon odor and tactile experiences in their early weeks that will either make them feel safe or in danger. Even though they lack language, they are 100% present and are absorbing everything around them. Are they feeling safe? They can't tell us, so we have to do our best and pay attention.

The anger we feel as adults makes most people uncomfortable because of personal issues, whether we are the "expresser" or the recipient of the anger. Our childhood fears are being triggered all the time. If you are the recipient, it may feel as if your world is crumbling. If you want to express yourself but don't feel safe to do so, you will hold back, and that suppression will surface somewhere else, either as passive aggression, displaced anger, physical maladies, shame, or emotional deadness.

SOME TYPICAL SCENARIOS:

- "Stop crying, or I'll give you something to really cry about!" This is our caregiver's attempt to stifle our anger.

- "If you don't stop crying, no dessert!" This is an attempt to bribe us.

- The silent treatment — what they give us by ignoring us, another form of manipulation.

- Whenever we express ourselves, our parents contradict us by saying: "Oh, that's not *really* what you mean…"

MARGO

Margo was the youngest in a large family. When she got get angry as a very young child, everyone teased her, which would make her even angrier. Her needs were being ignored.

One day, she got so frustrated when she was angry that she started to cry. As a result, she got picked up and held like a baby. She liked that. She was getting the attention she wanted — and deserved. All kids deserve attention.

She imprinted somewhere inside herself:

Anger + Crying = Attention

Now, when she cries, she sabotages her anger and acts powerless, yet it stops the show and everyone focuses on her tears, a form of manipulation.

A more effective method would be for her caregivers to take her into the next room, sit quietly with her, give her their presence and patience, dialogue with her on her level — and talk her through what's bothering her. Giving her vocabulary can start very young and give her a sense of power through verbal communication. A critical piece in one's socializing is learning the difference between feeling something and the behavior resulting from that feeling. Attempting to squelch a young child's anger only gives that child confusing messages. Acknowledging a child's anger in a calm, non-reactive way reinforces her self-esteem. Teaching children appropriate behavior instills confidence. Allowing them to vent, while staying within boundaries, helps them build trust.

> *Anger is a clue. It gives dimension to an otherwise flat voice. It will always tell us when we have been betrayed, disrespected, or violated. How Does Anger Connect to Money?*

How we express our anger is directly related to our self-esteem and self-worth. These two elements are the building blocks of one's life, and if they are skewed, every relationship will be distorted — whether it's with a person, a dog, food, alcohol or money. The truth is that your life will be managed by distortion, which I feel sure is not what you want. How you value yourself will be expressed in the visible, physical world — whether you are fully aware of it or not. This is why awareness is important.

Abandonment:
The Underlying Fear

If survival is the primary human driving force, then a dependent child who is pushed away intentionally through anger or neglect would have good reason to panic. "Who will meet my needs?" "Who will protect me?" "Who will help me survive?" Quite a question for a three-year-old.

Fear of abandonment is a learned behavior. It's a reaction to the withdrawal of affection and bonding. In attempting to establish a way to survive while remaining below the radar, a young child will create an adapted persona. That child will deeply bury authentic, creative energy while, at the same time, trying to anticipate and interpret the moods and actions of those around them. That child is no longer herself. She is doing what she feels is necessary to survive.

> *We need attachments in order to survive, even if those attachments are abusive and neglectful.*

A child will hang on to any shred of contact in order to get basic needs met. In some cases, that attachment feeds the illusion: "Maybe someday, they will realize how wonderful I am and love me for *me*." Fear of abandonment is the Super Bowl of emotions. This life force underlies every negative emotion. It is extremely potent because every species needs to bond — for food, water, shelter, and companionship. At times it can feel like a life-and-death struggle. Lack of bonding leads to isolation — for animals as well as humans. The story of the 130-year-old tortoise and the baby hippo that bonded after the Kenyan coast tsunami in 2004 is a textbook example of the need and drive to bond. The baby hippo was separated from his mother, so when he saw the giant male tortoise, which was moving, he started to follow it around and ended up nuzzling and hugging the reptile.

Every person needs a connection in order to survive. As children get older and develop skills that give them more power, our desperation to bond softens; we have other needs as we grow up, and can get them met in other ways. But the primal sense of loss remains, like a door ajar, waiting for the "right" person to step through it.

A mother who abandons her child is the greatest rejecter of all. The child carries this rebuff throughout life, which tends to have a domino effect, touching all parts of that child's life. Whether the child is abandoned physically or emotionally, the scarring on the psyche is profound. Not to be loved by your own mother gives a clear message to the child: "You are not lovable." This is the trigger that creates a two-track life – one real, one false.

Abandonment damages a child's self-esteem so intensely, it is almost as if the mother has died. But in this case, the child keeps waiting for the mother to change her behavior, and can spend a lifetime chasing the unobtainable. As an adult, reaching an understanding that this has occurred takes time and patience. The journey of healing is one that is ongoing. You can choose to remain wounded and stuck, or heal and move forward. Which will it be for you?

> *Healing is hard work. It's messy, scary, and painful. We live in an accelerated time where everyone wants to pop a pill, look for sound bites — achieve comprehension, depth and change — and all before the sun goes down. Our emotional lives don't work that way, or that quickly. And we are too complicated for any*

> **computer to duplicate. The process of healing helps you become freer — liberated to finally have the chance to start living the fulfilling life you were intended to have.**

MONIQUE

Monique was already in her mid-60s when we met. She was born during World War II, and her father was stationed overseas. She was a first child, born to a mother who already had been damaged by her own mother, passing down her fears, insecurities and need to please her own mother. And, Monique was a twin.

People are always surprised when I talk about twins who lack intimacy, the additional layer of damage a child walks around with when rejected by a twin. It's hard to figure out who inflicts more damage by rejection, the mother or the sibling. And, ultimately, does it matter? What does matter is that damage has been done, and healing is needed.

When Monique and I started working together, her mother was still alive, which made her journey move faster than that of people whose mothers had already passed. She was able to see, in real time, how differently her mother communicated with each of them, treating them differently; so it's no surprise that one became more aggressive than the other, and that Monique's sister became the dominant one.

The rage Monique suppressed over the years looked like depression, her chronic health issues were not a surprise, and her ability to hold a steady job that would have given her financial stability was beyond her grasp.

Getting her to see that she did nothing wrong to warrant such rejection was a constant touchstone; every session we repeated that theme in one form or another. By gaining a vocabulary that simultaneously expressed her true feelings without disguise and allowed her to let go of her suppressed rage without inflicting pain on her mother and sister, she was able to move on and eventually keep steady employment.

How Does Abandonment Impact One's Finances?

If getting one's needs met is a driving force, then the fear of abandonment will temper and influence how one expresses those needs. The hidden agenda will always be this:

- Don't get too close to the fire, or you'll get burned.

- Don't be too visible, don't be too real, don't ask for too much.
- Don't risk alienating people so much, they will pack up and leave.

Can you see how this works? If you connect shame about money with the fear of abandonment, having money problems is what I call "collateral damage" — the secondary result of the primary cause.

Not having clear boundaries fuels the fire of fear and in many cases shows up in the handling of money. How you handle and treat your money is a mirror for what's happening internally. Money is the perfect gauge for how you're feeling and how you react when your triggers are activated.

Check your purchases and ask yourself what was going on or how you were feeling when you bought that dress or those shoes, or didn't pay that bill. Abandonment influences your choices and, most of the time, in a negative way. These choices lead to poor handling of your finances, sometimes so extreme and self-destructive that the sad result is bankruptcy or homelessness. And still, we think it's about the money, never stopping to focus on our tangled emotions.

Every person who has passed through the portals of The Financial Whisperer's® workshop has experienced underlying issues of abandonment. It's such a universal fear. Almost every dysfunctional issue sits atop the fear of being left behind, alone, and unloved.

> ***People with healthy self-esteem are less susceptible to the fear of abandonment. They trust their own judgments, their own instincts, and can make healthy decisions in all areas of their life, including their finances.***

Chapter 3:
Engagement of the Outside World

In my workshops, clients experience growth and amazing revelations about themselves as they start to reclaim their power. But I warn them, on that journey of healing, we often move two steps forward, and then one step back. But that's all part of the journey, especially when we're busy.

That said, let's take a look at some gophers, which have a lot of personality and are busy 24/7 — so busy that they don't always see what's happening around them.

This chapter is about how we interact with the rest of the world. Many of you are reading this book because you think that your financial issues are only about dollars and cents, when the truth is that they are about much more. The quality of how you communicate your needs to others provides a lot of clues about the pain you walk around with every day and, therefore, how you deal with all issues in your life, including money.

It's NEVER About The Money... Even When It Is

Nine gophers are visible one morning from your back porch. You fill in the holes thinking you are in the clear, and the next day six reappear, so you fill the holes again. The next day, four reappear. This is the perfect setup for self-sabotage. Just when we think we have cured an issue or solved a problem, it can reappear in another form. But if your self-awareness scout is on guard, it will catch the little devil and set it on the right path.

Engagement of the Outside World

Have you ever thought about the behavior you use to engage the outside world? Have you noticed whether it sometimes appears in the form of procrastination, manipulation, chaos, the drive for perfection and not keeping your commitments to yourself? Moving *outside* your self to help you look at how you communicate with others gives you a perspective that helps you choose your next behavior.

Procrastination:
Free Beer Tomorrow

Comical as it sounds, Chellie Campbell taught this to me when I took her Financial Stress Reduction® workshop[12], putting off today what you can do tomorrow. Tomorrow never comes because it's always a day away. Thank you, Annie.

Is your life in a constant state of delay? Have you asked yourself *why*? Could it be that it's because you need to do this and you need to do that, but you never start, and when you do, you don't follow through? If so, trust me — I know this

---

[12] http://www.chellie.com

from personal experience — you are experiencing procrastination. We all do it at one time or another.

There is a natural resistance we have when confronted with an unpleasant task — such as telling someone the truth we've been holding back for months, giving notice at a job we've been at for years, asking for a raise, confronting a co-worker who has been abusive. In our need to resist, and our desire to protect ourselves — we procrastinate.

Procrastination is about postponing an activity, but there's more to it than that. It has judgment attached to it. There is a pejorative undertone that never implies anything positive. Postponing an activity implies rescheduling, which is sometimes necessary and sometimes not. But we need to beware, because postponing could be interpreted as laziness, which also carries judgment. Often the two are used together: "Bob is so lazy. All he does is procrastinate."

Is there such a thing as positive laziness or positive procrastination? What's the difference between relaxing, downloading the day, zoning out in front of the TV after a taxing week, cutting the grass to avoid looking for a job, or not buying toilet paper when you are down to your last roll?

How do procrastination and self-commitment intersect?

Engagement of the Outside World

Sometimes we need permission to spend the day re-charging our batteries. Women typically never feel entitled to carve out time for ourselves. Our families have always come first. Having time to do things for ourselves, without judgment, is the key to a well-balanced life, which includes not being cranky and edgy because our needs are not being met.

Procrastination is a dicey topic. Judgments carry the message of "shoulds" which, when used in a negative way, squelch natural individuality. But, sometimes the "shoulds" are important and can benefit us: You *should* look for a job, you *should* drink water, you *should* floss your teeth. All the healthy "shoulds" make sense. The dogmatic ones are what stop us in our tracks: You *should* go to the baby shower (even though you cannot stand the mother-to-be). You *should* call your cousin (after all, she might leave you something in her will).

By looking more closely at the underlying possible dynamic, we see a constant theme — fear. Just as fear sits underneath most, if not all, of our challenging emotions, so it does for procrastination and laziness. They are disguises that we designed in our childhood for protection against the imagined "monsters in the closet."

Perish the thought that we can be our authentic selves. Clearly, we got the message when we were five years old that *who* we were was unacceptable. So, as our life went off track, we picked up momentum — in order to function — by playing the role of someone who *was* acceptable. We learned to *not* express our true feelings.

Children have very basic needs: to be held, listened to, fed, and kept warm with clothing and a dry place to sleep. Food, clothing and shelter are easy; but giving a child one's attention 100%, 24/7, is not so easy. If, however, parents do not give their child 100% of their attention when the child seems frightened or angry, the message the child receives is: your emotional needs are not important now.

> **Procrastination and laziness are symptoms of our five-year-old expressing herself.
> She is feeling afraid.**

That child does not have many ways to announce to the outside world that she is uncomfortable. Sometimes acting out — throwing tantrums, screaming, crying, and refusing to go to sleep or eat — is a child's way of announcing her discomfort. When her actions go unnoticed or get misinterpreted, she quickly learns that her real self doesn't matter, and so she begins to develop her false self, the self who learns to successfully operate on the wrong track. She may appear successful on the outside, but she is feeling misunderstood and unloved on the inside — by others and even more so, by herself.

When a child's feelings are not validated, that child will assign his or her feelings to an external expression that the parent does not find threatening. For example, a child may learn that if he cries when he's angry, he will get picked up. If a child doesn't obey, she will get yelled at. In their system, negative attention is better than none at all.

Procrastination is a cousin to "Lack of Permission." When we do not give ourselves permission to occupy the next moment in our authentic, true self, we may appear lazy to the outside world.

> *If no one treats children with respect, they have no model for self-respect. Respect is the building block for trust. When self-respect shows up, procrastination takes a holiday.*

If you pay your bills late, wait until the last minute to transfer money, or pay your mortgage on the last day of your grace period, your relationship with money is crying — crying for help, because part of you is angry and no one is listening, not even you. When you stop listening to yourself, you are at the pinnacle of self-denial and your life suffers, especially your relationship to money. Look at your money for a moment and see what the trails of money crumbs are telling you. You may be in denial, but your money isn't. Money is always authentic; it never lies.

ANNE

Anne could not do one of the traditional steps necessary to be taken seriously in business: order business cards. Sounds simple, doesn't it? But it took her four months. She also could not get life insurance for her family. She just got health insurance two years ago. She is 39 years old with two children, and her internal engine could not "trespass" arenas that appeared adult-like without permission. So she appeared to be a procrastinator. And she was. But *why?*

She grew up in a home with no boundaries, no model for self-respect, and with parents who themselves were wrapped up in shame and a lot of chaos. Her father was overly controlling, which undermined her confidence, and yet, he was permissive about other parts of their lives. This was very confusing for a young child. Anne's monster in her closet was her father.

Anne was confident about giving her own children boundaries and support. When she looked in the mirror at her external choices versus her internal feelings, she was able to start with baby steps, pushing herself forward to procrastinate less and feel good about checking things off her daily list of tasks. Ordering business cards was at the top.

Because the fears that held her back were ingrained by the time she was five years old, and now manifested themselves in avoiding keeping commitments to herself, taking baby steps helped her feel less afraid of moving forward. She was able to tackle and complete tasks, and then scratch them off her list.

What baby step can you take today to help you feel that you're moving forward?

Manipulation:
Masking the Truth

We are all masters of manipulation. It's a form of emotional blackmail[13], hiding what our true needs are. You've manipulated others, haven't you? And you've been manipulated, too, right? We learn this form of communication from birth by copying what we experience with our parents and siblings. Monkey see, monkey do.

Conversely, when children are raised with respect and demonstrate differences that are celebrated, they are accustomed to being clear about what their needs are. This does not mean that they always get their requests met, but it does mean that they are heard and taken seriously.

> *Acknowledgment of one's needs is a clear statement that someone is listening and someone cares.*

---

[13] *Psychology Today* magazine Sept. 20th, 2009 Carl E. Pickhardt

Engagement of the Outside World

Children can often "read" their parents better than parents know their own children, odd as that sounds. Young children, for the most part, have no hidden agendas. They are innocent and pure. The manner in which they are socialized is what throws them off track. They develop an adapted persona to mask their authentic selves, so they can survive their environment.

Getting one's needs acknowledged is fundamental for a young child to feel whole, visible, and to have an intact sense of self. What and how children feel *is* their identity.

It's not unusual for a child who comes from an unsafe environment to use manipulation as a primary method to get personal needs met. Such a child is totally unfamiliar with the concept of being direct and finds it too revealing, causing feelings of shame and vulnerability. Masquerading is easier and almost becomes a lifestyle. These young children grow up with a finely tuned antenna, trying to pick up clues before they act. Their eyeballs can hear, their ears can feel the energy shift, and their noses can sniff the changes of wind, much like the female wolf trying to protect her pack.

Psychologist Elaine Aron, in her book series on *The Highly Sensitive Person in Love*[14], comments that people who are polarized into being "highly sensitive" have a harder time expressing their needs in a direct and clear fashion; they are more secretive and prone to avoid situations that may call them out of the shadows. They tend to isolate more and spend more time emotionally evaluating new people and circumstances before joining in.

Manipulation is a very sophisticated dance step, and a pre-selected partner (a parent) becomes an unwitting pawn in the tango. The irony is that parents are actually responsible for this distorted form of communication. Early on in their child's development, they did not make that child feel safe, they did not take their child's separateness as a positive step; instead, they found it threatening and protected themselves. Siblings will make the stew even murkier. But that's another story.

There are seven typical behaviors of emotional extortion:

---

[14] Aron, Elaine N. *The Highly Sensitive Person in Love: Understanding and Managing Relationships.* New York, NY: Crown Publishing Group, Broadway Books, 2000.

Engagement of the Outside World

Passive – Aggressive

This behavior diverts attention from the actual issue to acting as if some "wrong" has been committed. In fact, the behavior is actually masking anger — such behavior as withholding affection, pouting, screaming at the dog, acting apathetic. Saying "yes" when "no" is what you feel, or "no" when under calmer circumstances you might be saying "yes." Clouding our true feeling gives us the illusion of control in the hope that the other person will "get" it. It's also a great attention magnet for people who do not trust themselves to be clear about what they want.

People Pleasers

These people are sensitive to approval from others. Their instant reaction when there is a slight whiff of disapproval is: "Oh my God, I think he's mad at me!" The need for acceptance then distorts what they really feel and want. They will be hyper-vigilant to any subtle mood shifts in the people around them.

Rejecters

These people often are critical of others and reject them before they themselves can be the targets of rejection. They act angry, wronged, injured, almost to the point of indignation. They create this cloud of cause and effect: "If you don't come to Thanksgiving dinner, everybody will be disappointed." The truth being: "I have an agenda that needs to get met...it's about *me*, not you and not what you want."

Protecting One's Sense of Adequacy

These people can be manipulated by challenging their character. A father who harbors strains of not being attentive enough to his children will have an opening in his fence, a place where when he fails to do something, his child can criticize him for not being a good enough dad, playing on his already existing sense of inadequacy.

Guilt

This is the number-one card everybody plays at one time or another. It's a door that swings both ways. If the parents will convey to the child that unless he does what's requested, for them, *his* life will be altered. Young children do the same with their parents; they insist that unless they get their way, they will be unhappy, and even scarred for life.

Apathy

This removal of one's presence, more emotional than physical, touches off an acute sense of abandonment, which is the source of all angst. At the end of the day, what we all want is to feel valued and wanted, the missing link in our early childhood. Apathy is conveyed as if the relationship does not matter, therefore, we don't matter. We don't exist.

Intimidation

Intimidation is the precursor of all these behaviors; in and of itself, it can be a doozy. When a parent, and then a child, has a meltdown, it can be scary — especially when the child witnesses a parent going through it. Since there is no safe place for the child to hide, she learns to retreat into a private space, a bedroom, the parts of the brain that help remove her self from the moment. Ergo, as such children grow up, they have difficulty being in the moment because when that "in the moment" situation happened as a child, it was too scary.

Much of our lives we spend in reflection rather than introspection, which, in the moment is having what's in front of us be exactly what we need to learn and heal from. *From* is the key word here — moving away *from* the damage we experienced and imprinted on our brains as a young child — and looking *within* so that we can move *toward* healing thoughts.

> ***The remedy as adults? Build self-respect by being in the moment, direct and honest about your needs, and letting go of the outcome; by not trying to control another person to do what you want via a disguise of your authentic self.***

As we gain self-respect, which ushers in self-trust, we gain confidence and clarity. This demands that we be clear about our desires without judgment, without apology; in fact, that process becomes the cornerstone of our identity.

THE MANIPULATION OF ROBERT

Robert's parents are in their late 80s and he has a brother who is an alcoholic and refuses to go to AA, denying that he has an issue. His parents are constantly trying to make him feel guilty and to be more involved with the family. His sister lives across the country and another brother lives in

Engagement of the Outside World

Northern California. His mother constantly complains about her health and even has accused him of being a neglectful son. He shops for them every week and takes her to get her hair done weekly as well. He feels ashamed to say that sometimes he wishes they would just "go" and leave him in peace — and then he's afraid of the day that will happen, leaving him feeling even more alone.

This family lives with secrets. The fact that his brother denies that he has an issue sends a message to the entire family that they feel shame and wish they could hide it under the rug. And that protecting him is more important than Robert's needs. It's no wonder he feels so much rage that he's pushed to fantasies of them "moving on."

His constant state of aloneness and isolation has been with him forever, despite a 15-year marriage. When a child does not feel celebrated for being who he is and valued for being an individual, separate from others in the family, he starts to shut down. No one is meeting his needs and nurturing him in a way that makes him feel whole. He needs to start giving himself permission to have his own needs — and getting them met. The irony is: Even if he lived with his parents, his mother would still accuse him of being neglectful.

Chaos:
The Enemy of Logic

What does how we live say about who we are — and what really goes on in our internal world?

Our environment — whether it's our car, bedroom, or home — gives our inner five-year-old a chance to make a statement about finances, food, choice of friends, partners, family connections and career interactions.

What are we saying now that we could not (or were not allowed to) express so many years ago? People who have financial challenges sometimes hide beneath physical conditions. A messy environment or one that's too neat can signal a call for help; there may not be enough control over another kind of suffocating behavior — perfectionism.

There is a certain visual logic that goes on in one's environment. Papers need to be stacked with some order, jackets hung up, shoes get put away; anything that has a corner, such as newspapers, magazines, books, require some alignment. When objects are in order, we feel we have control. Opening a closet and finding clothes hanging with pants together, blouses by color, jackets by tone, gives us calmness and peace.

> **We can see our reflection only in still waters.**

Chaos is your inner five-year-old expressing her fears, her anger, her panic, or her shame. She is having a tantrum, and the chaos will keep you spinning, in a fog, holding you back from being in the moment, preventing clarity from guiding you to make the best choice for you. Chaos has a real function. It's not an accidental occurrence; it happens by design. The need to pretend *not* to be able to get control reflects not having control as a child, having no power, getting no respect for having different feelings. Chaos is disguised anger. The mess is screaming: "Help me...look at me!"

SALLY

Sally's nickname was PigPen, after the endearing and confused friend of the cartoon character Charlie Brown. Her family had given her that name. Her sister was called String Bean because she was a very tall adolescent, her younger brother had been dubbed Four-Eyes because he wore glasses at an early age, and her other sister was tagged Ruby because of a bright red birthmark on her chest. Not a very kind family.

Sally's purse was disorganized, and her car was littered with empty soda cans, food wrappers, and papers strewn all over. Her house was cluttered with piles of newspapers, laundry not yet put away, dishes in the sink, and a medicine cabinet that spewed overstocked shelves every time someone opened it.

It's no surprise that she had difficulty managing her finances, for they too were chaotic. She went into a panic every time an expense arose that she could not cover easily — such as new tires, a visit to the vet for her dog, or a broken tooth.

Another sign of her internal discomfort was her constant laughter at apparently nothing. She ended sentences with a giggle, and had difficulty maintaining eye contact with anyone with whom she spoke.

In our work we were able to piece together that while growing up, she felt invisible. Her younger brother had received most of the attention because he was five years younger than she was and nine years younger than the oldest. He was the baby and they treated him as such. An older

Engagement of the Outside World

sister had chronic health issues that siphoned off the parents' attention, and the eldest child always acted as the third parent. The message Sally got loud and clear was: "Your needs have to fit in. We don't have time for you to want differently. You will get what we give you — and you should be grateful for that."

Sally's childhood home life was so chaotic that one day, when Sally was five years old, the family left the house while Sally was in the bathroom and no one noticed that she was missing for two hours.

She constantly felt like the black sheep of the family — always lamenting: "Where do I belong?" Her need to constantly re-enact her anxiety as a young child kept her locked on a treadmill, repeating that old pattern because it was familiar. Changing that behavior, in her subconscious, meant she would be rejected again, abandoned again.

We created a "homework" assignment for her — a short list of things to do daily, to make her behavior accountable. The intent was to attempt to flush out that inner five-year-old who was creating self-sabotage, so that she could address those fears she had at a young age, as well as her five-year-old's need for attention.

PERFECTION:
THE JOURNEY WITHOUT A DESTINATION

We addressed perfection a bit in the prior chapter. One might assume that perfection and chaos had very different core messages, but in fact they are two sides of the same coin.

Perfection thrives on the illusion that some day parental love can finally be won. Chaos thrives on negative attention: better to be scolded than ignored. In the middle of the two extremes there is calmness through order — calmness that springs from respect of the property and of the tenant. When the environment is clean, visually things make sense and don't cry out: "Don't touch me!" It looks lived in without being messy, out-of-control or sterile. The owner is calm and does not make excuses about why the house is a mess, because it's not. It's peaceful; all the possessions and objects know they are being cared for, they feel secure, and so does the owner. And this calmness extends to the owner's wallet.

> ***Treating money with respect is the same as treating your house with respect.***

Engagement of the Outside World

The drive for perfection is learned early in one's childhood as a misconception, that if we are "perfect," we will be loved. But in fact, perfection is a shame-based drive. It removes one from the moment, reduces playfulness and the feeling of freedom. It has no feeling of safety. The drive goes into infinity, floating without boundaries, a very different experience from excellence.

> ***Excellence is fueled by enjoyment.***
> ***Perfection is fueled by fear.***

The need for perfection can sometimes signal the need for constant self-evaluation and the almost obsessive drive to defend one's self against comparison. This need completely shuts down all creativity.

It also discounts feedback from others that might counter one's pre-determined experience — feedback that might shed some light. But instead we hear only the negative and dismiss the positive. This behavior cements our inability to trust our instincts because they are undermined by the drive to get things "right."

Perfection-driven people can never be "wrong." They hold themselves to a rigid standard and are intolerant of having any flaws. And yet, they feel so much shame all the time that they assume they are continuously wrong. Their environment is meticulous, bordering on sterile. You will never see a coffee cup in the sink. They are hypersensitive to any changes around them, always living in the fear mode. Another clue is that they can be unforgiving and unwilling to let go — that somehow forgiving someone is to admit self-defeat and would require tolerance, or a bending of the "rules." They live with a lot of rules, the kind that go beyond not wearing white after Labor Day.

A child's entire focus, when perfection-bound, is on performance. This robs them of the joy of the process. The activity is external, visible and quantifiable. Perfection is a soulless monster; no matter how perfect the action, perfection-driven people are never, ever satisfied. Nothing is good enough. There is no rest for these weary souls, as they walk a treadmill that never stops moving.

Tanya

Tanya's drive for perfection bordered on Obsessive Compulsive Disorder (OCD). She came from a family that was very sports-focused and less attentive to her personal needs. She was extremely competitive in soccer, basketball, and softball, and won constantly.

She connected the accolades with affection, but the focus was on her accomplishments, not on her attempts. As a result, she always felt empty. Winning became everything.

Also, she was uncomfortable with short men. When I met Tanya, she was dating a man she was absolutely crazy about, but could not take him seriously because he was shorter than she was. "Not marriage material," she told me.

We were able to piece together that his being shorter created this pedestal feeling inside her. His looking up to her literally made her feel as if he could not see her clearly, so she could not trust that he could really see her for who she was inside, only the outside packaging. She seemed to relate this to the trophies in her bedroom, something that was *about* her, an event, not something about *who* she was.

Understanding that piece of the puzzle freed the monster in her closet. She is now engaged to him, and wears three-inch heels when they go out.

> ***Our lives are more about the journey and the opportunities we are given to heal than the literal challenge in front of us.***

It's NEVER About The Money… Even When It Is

How Perfection Relates to Finances
Perfectly Imperfect

Tory is 45 years old. She spends more than she earns, and even though the closet store she owns is doing okay in a bad economy, she awakes at 3:00 AM in a cold sweat. With two kids in college, she's been a single parent since her kids were ages two and four. A college attended by one of her children is very expensive. She worries about asking her son to switch colleges if she can't continue to pay for it. She does not want him to get a student loan.

She is a self-admitted "straightener"; every corner needs to be at right angles, everything needs to be in descending or ascending order. Because her children have pointed it out to her, she's aware that she's always correcting everyone's grammar. She's aware that she's on a continual worry treadmill and wants to get off.

It's not lost irony that Tory should be in the closet business — a wonderful metaphor for our internal lives. She reminds me of a friend of mine who has to be perfect *all* the time, whether it's her handwriting style, her lingerie drawer, the utensils in her state-of-the-art kitchen or her inability to leave the house without make-up, ever.

Tory feels out of control and experiences a lack of boundaries, which gets played out in the financial arena. Underneath that anxiety sits the lack of trust.

Let's assume you have the drive for perfection, defined as one who needs to have order *all* the time, without exception, and anything less than order creates anxiety or, at the very least, is very distracting. The need to be perfect usually comes from an unavailable mother and a father who could have also been unavailable, judgmental, critical, or remote, so that there was no opportunity to find balance. There also could have been the appearance of attention but no real intimacy, which would confirm to children that they were not valued for *who* they were, but rather *what* they did — their accomplishments.

Sometimes these children are involved in sports, spelling bees, or other competitive experiences, because in that dynamic, children have the false assumption that *if* they win the trophy, they are winning their parents' approval — and, therefore, love. This is the hamster on the wheel, constantly in motion but getting nowhere, because it's an illusion.

If children do not receive needed attention and nurturing by their ninth month, chances are they won't ever get it in the form in which they desperately need it.

How Do We Fix This?

Feeling in control can sometimes be the recognition that no matter what happens, you will be okay, you will be intact despite that what may be unfolding in front of you seems daunting.

Trusting that feeling is, in part, what you're missing. What you look at today has been shaped by your childhood experiences.

> ***Your fears sit on situations that happened long ago, that are recurring today only because you choose to see them through your childhood anxieties. The thing is, you now have the power that you lacked as a 10-year-old.***

So that child, who believed that she could win her mother's love by winning trophies and getting A+'s, is still in pain, still waiting for the love to finally arrive. By living in the false belief, she distorts her current reality, which is: She *would* have the money and resources to pay for her children's college if she were to manage her income better. She *would* be able to make choices by creating healthy projections and decisions, rather than those based on fear.

Chapter 4:
Getting Control

This Roadmap is the Holy Grail. It is the road out. It is the single most important tool in your toolbox. The arrows go in only one direction. You cannot leapfrog the stations; you must start by keeping commitments to your self, which will allow you self-respect, then self-trust and self-love. This sounds easy, but it's not. The exercises you will read later are all designed to draw out your inner five-year-old so you can hear what she feels — which was ignored years ago.

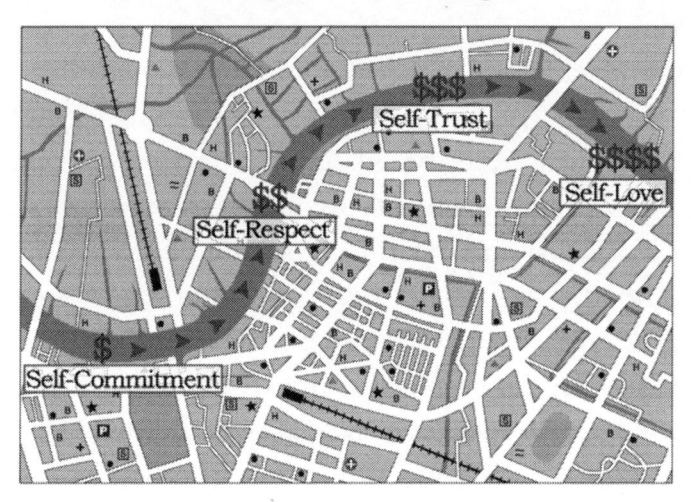

At the end of the day everything always comes down to control: Who wants it, who has it. How do we finally get control at this stage in our lives? We take control by setting boundaries, allowing ourselves to feel compassion, practicing patience and giving ourselves permission to do what needs to be done in order reach our destination, which is contentment.

Boundaries:
Protection for Our Individual Souls

The poet Robert Frost wrote: "Good fences make good neighbors." Boundaries are about mutual respect. They define where you stop and someone else begins, and create a clarity about everyone's needs.

Children need defined boundaries in order to feel secure. They rely on their caregivers to make decisions on their behalf — not that they really have a choice when they are very young, but that's the whole point. Looking back at my childhood, we had no boundaries, which supported a toxic environment.

Children have no preconceived notions, only an imagination fed by films, books, TV, and social interactions. They are sponges, absorbing everything and then copying everything their caregivers do. It's a sobering thought, isn't it? They trust whoever tells them that Santa comes down the chimney. In those innocent windows of learning, their expectations of tomorrow are formed and reinforced.

When they live in an unstable environment, the lack of stability becomes predictable and opens the portal to fear of the unknown. A child who is brought up in an affirming, healthy environment will view the unknown as exciting and develop an adventurous spirit. For the rest of us who will heal later, the unknown can, at times, feel like emotional bungee jumping.

If, as adults, we have not created healthy boundaries, our inner child defines a certain reality, and then reacts to that fantasy. This reinforces our lives being off-track, making us feel like a fraud, and more often promotes self-loathing. Boundaries provide protection for our individual souls; when they're missing, the feeling of inner security is gone.

> ***Breaking free from misconceptions is the journey of self-discovery and healing.***

It's NEVER About The Money... Even When It Is

TANYA

Remember Tanya? She had the classic syndrome of first-born child needing to protect her mother. She was the oldest of five children born very close in age (within seven years of one another). Her mother had never healed from her own father's premature passing. Tanya's grandmother, who was living with them, turned to her daughter to run the house and make up for her loneliness in the loss of her husband. So, Tanya's mother became a caretaker when she was 12, not leaving much room to be a little girl.

It's not without irony that Tanya's mother had five children quickly and, of course, Tanya was pressed into helping instead of enjoying a carefree childhood.

Tanya was like a third parent. The boundary challenges came chugging down the track, right at her — powie! zowie! — she never knew what hit her; she was suddenly thrust into the caretaking model, making dinner, doing laundry, making lists for her siblings, perhaps loving the power but not realizing the poison it was creating in her system.

Tanya did not get her need for attention met. She made the assumption that if she made her mother happy, she would somehow get the attention she craved. Her inner desires created illusions and actions. She was pursuing an unattainable fantasy that was always beyond her grasp. Tanya could not distinguish between what was appropriate for her and what belonged to her parents. She acted like the model child and repressed her own needs to be seen as an individual.

Tanya's confusion over deserving money led her to appear to be an underachiever. How incongruent was it that this star athlete, who won many trophies, couldn't win at the money game? The shame her own mother had lived with got passed on to Tanya. Shame-bound parents have no boundaries. They are forever projecting onto their child their own needs and illusions. Children get swept up in that turbine of confusion, which eliminates and undermines their authentic selves.

> **Having boundaries helps children who are perfection-driven. Clarity of who they are and who they are not is critical for their sense of confidence.**

When a child expects confusion and lack of stability, everything seems scary and out of reach. That child doesn't trust himself, because his caregivers never affirmed to him that he was okay, and that he was valued for just being himself. In his small world, the only thing he can be sure of is that nothing is safe.

Healthy boundaries, on the other hand, keep our lives on a single, forward-moving track. Healthy boundaries, especially when one has young children, will provide sanity and a positive role model for those children, so their world is predictable in ways that build their self-esteem.

Can You Give Your Kids Too Much Truth About Money?

Roxie grew up in a household where secrets and holding things back was frowned upon. The order of the day was to be always candid and transparent. They talked about money — having it or not — very openly. Roxie now has two young children of her own and does the same with them.

In her marriage, she acts the same — says what she thinks and feels in the moment, even when she's angry and even if her children are present. She thought this was the healthy thing to do until recently she read an article about the damage such direct honesty can inflict on young children in the same home environment. So now she's confused. Should she be a truth teller or not? When her kids ask for new sneakers, she says, "No, your Dad's commission check was smaller this month." Is that wrong?

It's a mother's primary responsibility to create and maintain an environment that makes her children feel safe and secure. Boundaries that make sense provide safety. If you grew up in an environment without boundaries, you have a hard time differentiating between what information your children can manage and what will make them feel insecure.

Financial issues in a family need to be between parents, without involving the children, except for discussions that are instructional in nature. It's also a mother's responsibility to model respect. How she treats her children's needs and celebrates their individuality starts very early on. It needs to be consistent with the way she treats their father, even if he doesn't live in the same house.

Expressing your anger with your partner, disguised as you might think it is, makes your children nervous and insecure. Children are hypersensitive to mood shifts and pick up on the slightest change that adds either to their sense of safety or feeling that they're living in a war zone. A lack of boundaries will make children question their own value and sense of competence. It's not uncommon for them to immediately believe that the mood shift is their fault. Parents who are at odds with each other need to always put their children's perception first, so they stay grounded.

Compassion:
A Sense of Forgiveness

Have you noticed how some people are spontaneously kind and always seem to come from a place of compassion and tolerance? They would never ignore a short person in the grocery store trying to reach for something high up. They would never ignore an elderly person looking confused on a street, or a mother pushing a stroller with many kids running through an intersection. How do you fit in this picture?

Where does compassion come from? Is it a learned behavior or is it innate? How do we sometimes have it for others but lack it for ourselves?

How do we embrace it for ourselves when, for most of our lives, we have lived with impatience, self-loathing and shame?

For those of us who have to learn it later in life, it becomes a learning curve based on our humanity. To be applied to our selves, it must tie to our ability to forgive our families, our circumstances and ourselves.

What is compassion? A wise person once said, "It is the opening of the heart in the moment, allowing ourselves to feel empathy for what is before us." *Webster* compares it to sympathy, tenderness, sensitivity, and charity.

When I work with clients, I give them the metaphor of a Hershey's candy bar: taking one small bite at a time when one is trying to shift from the constant hamster wheel of being self-critical to finding humor in choices or circumstances. It's a challenge for them to not take everything as an indictment of character.

> ***The process is a slow unfolding of tightly wound constraints, taking them a moment at a time, a bite at a time, and setting realistic goals that are not about failing, but are about getting rewarded for trying — and trying again.***

At some point, the veneer we created years ago to protect ourselves starts to crack and chip away, one bite-sized piece at a time.

How does compassion feed permission? In observing so many clients and people over the years, I have found that there always seems to be a prevalent undercurrent of the *need* to get permission to meet one's needs. Almost as if having needs must be justified. Why do people have so much difficulty allowing themselves to put *their* wishes first, at least some of the time?

So often we find an excuse to beat ourselves up. Who gets to decide when that is the appropriate response? What is a reasonable amount of time for self-punishment when we have done something wrong? Whose needs are really being met by self-punishment? Do we all live with a secret dream of boundary-less perfection that can never be obtained, that ignites when we try to get our needs met and results only in our feeling shame or guilt? Who, in our early years, set the stage for perfection?

Accepting ourselves as flawed, with clay feet, requires letting go and trusting the intangible. In the absence of clarity, our authentic self gets distorted and abandoned, but can be retrieved through focus and humored discipline.

We all prefer humored discipline. Mary Poppins had it right, "a spoonful of sugar helps the medicine go down."

PAM

Pam's mother was unhappy and unfulfilled, and she passed that emotional deadness onto her children. Growing up Pam was the model child, or at least she tried to be. She did everything she could to please her mother, but to no avail. Her mother's subtle and overt rejection put Pam on a perfection-seeking path that created intolerance for herself. As an adult, Pam was self-loathing. It's no surprise that she didn't have any close friends and that she assumed every woman she saw at the supermarket was happy. That assumption made her feel diminished, and it contributed to her feeling that "they had it all," and that she was worthless.

Soon after we started working together, she changed her assumptions; when she saw attractive women, she learned to tell herself they were, in fact, struggling with husband issues, financial woes, and that they hadn't spoken to their mothers in five years. Conversely, when she saw people she did not think were attractive or rich, she also created stories about them that made her feel more compassionate and kind toward them. These small little exercises helped Pam get some space between her constant self-loathing and also provided a reality check: Everyone is flawed and no one has it easy. Creating stories can be a great path to healing and getting control of your downward spiraling mood.

We all need to be more kind to ourselves. We have to have faith in the universe. Faith is not about religion; it's about trusting the intangible. Faith is running full steam ahead with your eyes closed, trusting that the ground will come up to meet the next falling foot. Faith is a spiritual commitment that gets tested all the time. Experiencing ourselves fully gives us the capacity to have faith. When we come from a place of joy and abundance, compassion feels natural.

How Do Compassion and Finances Connect?

Take a step back. Get some perspective. You are doing the best you can right now. You need to accept that none of what happened to you as a child was your fault. Your task at hand, in the present, is to get to know yourself in a way you never had permission to do before. You are on this huge learning curve about your favorite person — you. You are more interesting than any apps, any computer program, any movie star. You are unique and special, so much so that if they had to cast someone to play you in a film, they could not find anyone *but* you.

Your financial issues are symptoms of the problem. Solve the problem, and your financial concerns will shift. Remember the crack in the hub of the wheel in Chapter 1? Heal the cracked hub, and everything will move smoothly. Having compassion gives you breathing space about your finances.

Commitment:
A Contract for Future Action

When I am working with a new client, I usually ask: "On a scale of 1 to 100%, how are you on keeping commitments to the outside world? And how are you at keeping commitments to yourself?" Most of the time, the answer is: "100% to the outside world, and 40% to myself." There are those times when the answer is: "100% to both." But I know that, regardless, the root is the same, only the tools to heal are different. When someone keeps commitments to him or herself 100%, he or she is a walking powder keg, on a tightrope that can snap at any moment. There is zero tolerance to make a mistake, but he or she, too, can shift and heal.

I define commitment as a contract for future action — creating something that is predictable which then will allow trust to be a foundation upon which everything rests. But the breaking of that contract confirms to the other party that someone cannot be relied upon, cannot be trusted to show up. Either way, it creates a track record for an assumption: What this person says and what this person does are two different things.

Keeping a commitment is a matter of respect — to others, when we have promised to take care of something, and to ourselves, to uphold the inner integrity to *be* who and what we say we are.

Respect is the single most important factor in building a child's self-esteem. And it all begins with a parent treating a young child's feelings with that respect. The way we treat other people is echoed in our environment — the respect we show to family, friends, neighbors and fellow human beings in general. Mutual respect is a way of life. This is where respect and boundaries intersect — understanding what belongs to whom, and what doesn't.

> **What stops us from keeping self-commitments? Laziness? Too many things to do in not enough time? Not being able to set priorities? The real reason is fear — fear of eclipsing the monsters in our closets.**

Monsters represent our childhood fears, which were imprinted by the time we were five years old. Monsters are the assumptions we deduced from the reactions to our behaviors from our parents and siblings, all of which contributed to living our lives on two tracks. The fear is about abandonment; we were abandoned once, we do not want to be abandoned twice. That assumption — that we will be abandoned again — can have a lifelong grip on us until we have the self-awareness to break the cycle.

In the very first session I have with people, no one has ever asked me to define self-commitment, because their internal compass understands the word and the shame or discontent they feel when not keeping their word to themselves. Not keeping self-commitments is self-sabotage, which is a self-preservation device created while we are on the adapted-self track. Self-sabotage makes us negotiable and will short-circuit our path to our goals by allowing our fears to dance inside us unchecked.

How do we break out of our glass cage? How do we get from self-sabotage to self-respect? You can't learn to swim while on the sofa. You need to be in the water, the muck, and the challenge, in order to get your inner five-year-old to come forth and be experienced.

> ***The only way to break this cycle is to coax your five-year-old out of the shadows and give her what she never received — patience and presence.***

Here's a tool you can use:

- Start by assigning small simple tasks, like daily flossing, drinking more water, getting more exercise, staying away from sugar, cutting back on alcohol. Watch, as if you are outside yourself, how the resistance starts inside you with that little internal voice dismissing the assignment, as if it's not important.

- Then have your inner five-year-old sit on your lap and tell you why she cannot go for a walk *now*...or floss those teeth, *now*. Look right into her eyes and give her your patience and presence. That's how you start to break the cycle. You prove to your inner five-year-old that you *can* and *will* take care of her...that she can trust you...right now.

There is a progression that moves forward from keeping self-commitments to gaining self-respect, which then feeds self-trust and the ultimate, self-love.

On the other side of this coin are people who are perfection-driven, always keeping commitments to themselves and to others, 100% of the time. And yet, they are unhappy, they lack self-confidence (even if they act arrogant) and move through the world unable to trust others. While they do show up, they are not really present — always on guard, always waiting for the other shoe to drop. They cannot be intimate and cannot allow others to be close to them. They hover. They live their lives on a treadmill, always in motion but never arriving at their destination.

The outside world is always surprised to hear that a person has declared bankruptcy, or done something out of character because no one ever really saw the pain beyond the façade, the signs that something didn't fit.

We all struggle with self-commitments, which is why permission becomes a huge healing tool. Permission gives us the green light to be ourselves, to accept our feelings, to take actions that reinforce to ourselves that we can be whole; we can be separate and still survive and thrive. We don't need others to define who we are — our feelings do that for us.

Our feelings are our identities; attempting to stifle them in a young child sends the message that *who* we are is unacceptable, that we need to change in order to be approved of and loved. These are the voices of the monsters in our closet.

As we have learned, regardless of our age, we are entitled to our feelings. What we do with those feelings is part of our socializing, part of our instructions from the material world on *how* to proceed. A child will mimic older siblings, parents and caregivers on how to behave. This gets very confusing when the parents say one thing and do something different. Kids get confused, which is a breeding ground for a lack of trust and lying. It's also confirmation that in order to survive, we have to do what we're told.

Keeping Self-Commitments Is the Key to Healing

In challenging economic times, many of us see a path to more healing, and more opportunities to move away from toxic elements in our lives, even when they exist only in our minds — remnants of early childhood episodes of rejection.

Many of us read inspirational books on occasion, listen to recordings that sometimes sound as if they're providing new information, and promise ourselves we'll do better tomorrow. Then tomorrow arrives, and we are someplace else, forgetting our promise to ourselves.

> *Healing is a choice.*
> *When we choose not to shift our thoughts, not to gain perspective, we are basically telling ourselves we do not deserve better.*

You know what the comedy of it all is? We already have all the answers. We do. What we respond to when we read inspirational books is those writers' perspectives when we're lost in that dark tunnel of confusion about who we *really* are, and what we *really* want. That conflict keeps us small, keeps us in the shadows. Then, we hear what we *think* are profound words and say to ourselves: "Ah-ha!" Those words we respond to are inspirational because we already *knew* what we are reading, but could not access it because fear stood in our way. What stops people from keeping self-commitments? Fear. Nothing but fear. Plain and simple — the fear that *if* we are to be seen for who we *really* are, we'll get thrown off the bus, fired from our job, rejected by our family or friends, and for a very young child, that feels like a death threat.

How does that apply when that child grows up, and is now 45? Unless that child has had enough experiences to repair self-esteem and low confidence, that fear appears as self-sabotage when making the choice to keep a commitment. Even something as simple as making the commitment to exercisc daily ends up being occasional rather than every day. Why couldn't that commitment be maintained? Because there's a fear of being successful, even in the smallest measure, which is often played out on a grander scale: not making enough money, not living up to one's full potential, living in the grip of the façade of powerlessness, not feeling competent.

All of our childhood dramas are played out on symbolic levels when we are older; what appears to be one thing can actually be something totally different. I grew up being afraid of frogs and lived in the countryside. The unpredictable movement of a jumping frog symbolized the unpredictable environment of my home. And our housekeeper promised us warts on our hands if we touched them — fear.

> **So how do we re-commit to making healthier choices? We choose to heal rather than stew in our own juices.**

We choose to stand up for ourselves, even in the face of possible terrible ramifications. We choose to *not* worry and instead trust the universe that things will be okay. We choose to trust ourselves. We earn that trust via self-respect, which begins with keeping our commitments to ourselves. The answer is that simple and clear: make different choices. Be aware that the bees have left the hive, even though, from a distance, it looks menacing. Upon closer inspection, we find that the hive is empty. We can consciously shift our behavior by choosing what and how to think.

Fears are rooted in our childhood, but we have blossomed beyond those years and *can* move on to make different choices now. Our bodies have moved on. Why not our minds?

Permission:
The Gift of Letting Go

If choice is the expression of true power, then permission, or entitlements, becomes a conduit to make it so. Permission is defined as authorizing change, giving freedom to what is restrained, and letting go.

This concept of *needing* permission is more common to women than men; men for the most part have an innate sense of entitlement resulting from the way their mothers nurtured them and from societal mores that continually reinforce that men have power. They are encouraged to be aggressive, forward-moving and on top.

Women grow up with a set of expectations that are different from those of men. As history has shown, men have most often led the charge and women have been the followers.

Since "Rosie the Riveter" emerged in WWII, women have taken on increasingly larger roles in the workforce and in politics. There has been a shifting of power from the one who has it to the one who needs it. Sometimes it takes a role model to set change in motion.

Several years ago, Oprah Winfrey went public about how she spends her Sundays — in her pajamas, relaxing and being a "couch potato." That story reverberated through the sleepwear industry; sales skyrocketed. Women were taking time for themselves to be self-nurturing without apology and taking care of themselves in ways they had only fantasized. Oprah, reaching millions of women within a one-hour program, was the catalyst.

Years ago I read a book that has become a classic in women's studies, *Women Who Run With the Wolves*.[15] It describes us in our authentic state: an Alpha female wolf shares many common traits with women: "Healthy wolves and healthy women share certain psychic characteristics: keen sensing, playful spirit and a heightened capacity for devotion. Wolves and women are relational by nature, inquiring and possessed of great endurance and strength. They are deeply initiative, intensely concerned with their young, their mate and their pack. They are experienced in adapting to constantly changing circumstances, they are fiercely stalwart and very brave."

---

[15] Estés, Clarissa Pinkola. *Women Who Run with the Wolves.* New York, NY: Random House, 1992.

In current societies, women are shaped and influenced by advertising, as well as the environment in which they grew up, and their genetic disposition. The world of advertising and early childhood environment often control, through guilt and shame, the enemies of permission.

> ***Anything that diverts our intrinsic drive away from what is natural to us diminishes our authenticity and self-worth.***

The seeds of disconnection from one's true self are planted when a child is an infant; how her needs are treated sets into motion what will then be considered her self-esteem. This positive, strong sense of self or damaged sense of self, will domino into adulthood and be reflected in the choices a woman makes. An authentic sense of self will be demonstrated in a confident woman. Conversely, a damaged sense of self will be reflected in further widening of the two tracks on which a person will travel and the adapted persona will continue to work on surviving, while her authentic self never sees the light of day.

It's NEVER About The Money... Even When It Is

Adults who need permission to get their own needs acknowledged come from a childhood of discarded instincts and suppression. A childhood environment of narcissism from parents and siblings constantly puts an adult into a quandary of whose needs come first. My spouse's needs or mine? My children's needs or mine? My dog's needs or mine? Where are the boundaries that offer sanity and release from guilt and shame? When will it be my turn to be seen and cherished for who and what I am?

CHLOE

Chloe has struggled with a mother who never allowed Chloe to be herself. When she started her sessions, Chloe had the disapproving voice of her mother in her head. She inherited from her mother a talent for storytelling and reminded me of Meryl Streep in the film *Out Of Africa*.

Chloe also wrote well. She inherited from her mother the message: "Never brag about yourself." So, Chloe could not distinguish between sharing her accomplishments and bragging — they sounded the same to her. She had written a screenplay, showed it to her mom, and her mother's response was: "Yes dear, that is a lovely hobby." Chloe didn't give herself permission to assert that her talent was not a mere hobby.

One of the many things Chloe learned in our sessions was that the voice of her mother in her head was fear-based. It was not her voice. She had inherited her mother's fears.

You *can* let go. Give yourself permission to experiment; share your accomplishments with total strangers, and see how no one laughs at you and that the world does not stop spinning. Don't rob your creative side of the energy it has to identify who you really are.

Permission and money? They go back to the fundamentals: Who has the power to *not* buy that latte? Who has the power to ask for a raise? Who has the power to determine your self-worth?

Answer: You do.

Chapter 5:
The Ultimate Goal

These Redcoats, snappy as they appear, represent alignment.

You may ask: "How will gaining self-awareness affect my money?" Money issues are what I call collateral damage, the result of something much deeper and older. So, as that older issue heals, so will everything else in the wagon wheel that you saw in Chapter 1.

The Redcoats move in unison — as one steps forward, the rest of the line follows. As you heal, all of your emotions will align, and you will feel better about yourself, and usher love and joy into your life. And isn't that what we all want? Isn't that the whole point of living this life?

The ultimate goal of stability — which not only embraces our finances, but also allows for love to flourish in its purest form — is the result of healing through self-awareness.

Collateral repair comes from self-awareness. It's what I call healing of the second tier issues, allowing us to live within our means, eat healthy, and receive and give love. All of this can happen but only if the center hub of our wheel is sturdy.

It's not an easy journey by any means. It's a choice we make when we are at the crossroads of change: Do we, or do we not examine what pushes us outside our comfort zone in order to reclaim entitlements from our childhood?

Healing:
The Compass of Feeling

How do we heal? How do we become the person we wish to be when the prospect of it seems an ocean away? How do we finally live our lives on one authentic track?

Now that you have reached this final chapter, you've received the message many times that you have more power than you choose to use. You have learned *why* all that has held you back is rooted in your early years and that everything now in front of you can serve as a symbol of your past experiences.

But what does it matter if you have all the information to heal but lack the tools to grab hold of your entitlements? That's the whole point. Other people have moved on with their lives, and are absorbed in their own issues, their own pain, and the monsters in their own closets.

Now is the time for you to take your place at the adults' table, perhaps even at the head of the table. This is your time to come out of the shadows and shine brightly — one candle at a time is fine.

> ***True healing is not an intellectual exercise. It comes from feeling, not thinking.***

If you can feel the pain, you can heal it. Identifying it and allowing it light and air takes courage that most people lack, so congratulate yourself if you want to continue and try some of the exercises proposed below.

It's NEVER About The Money... Even When It Is

SURVIVAL TIPS FROM THE FRONT LINES

(Movement toward the light requires focus, discipline and faith.)

- Identify what you want. Write it down. If you can't be clear, be patient. Believe (have faith) that the answer is waiting for you. The spiritual world moves ahead of the material world.

- If you feel antsy-urgency, STOP. Breathe deeply, calm down. Fear is creating the urgency. Clarity cannot spring forth if you are in motion. Remember? You can see your reflection only in still waters. Einstein said: "The side of your brain that created the problem is not the same side that will solve the problem."

Tools You Can Work With

- If you are a perfectionist, leave things undone. Leave dishes in the sink overnight, leave socks on the floor, and pay attention to the fact that nothing bad will happen if you do. You have made the decision to not do certain things. YOU have the power now.

The Ultimate Goal

- Sit with someone and create a real financial inventory. Look at the monthly expenses you'll need to cover for your children and yourself and look at where you can trim. You will be able to create this budget, however, only after you have started to make and keep commitments to yourself.

- Some of these commitments might be: Pick small things in your everyday life that maybe you don't do, but should do, such as: floss every night, drink water, journal, take time to be self-nurturing, exercise. Pick one to start. Do these things every day in the beginning. Or leave your environment in some disarray and resist the temptation to make it all neat and tidy. Keeping those small commitments when you feel the desire to do the opposite builds your control muscles, which leads to self-respect and self-trust.

- Pay attention to how you feel as you reach out to do something differently. What are the voices in your head saying to one another?

- If awakened at 3AM, what would be the key word to describe yourself, your number one trait? What would be your Achilles heel?

Remember, your journey is about learning who you are, so the sweetness goes with the bitter.

- If you feel lost and overwhelmed, STOP. Get centered and repeat the chant: "I am sorry, please forgive me, I love you." Have compassion for being human, and cut yourself some slack. Whatever happened in your childhood was never your fault.

- Sometimes, the best centering thing to do is to read a book you love for 20 minutes, without stopping. Carry it with you if you can.

- Everything starts with letting go, which is a shift in ownership. It's a shift in perception to see what is before you, from a different perspective, without trying to control the outcome. Remember the adage: "If you change the way you look at something, what you look at will change." Often it's about the ability to trust the unseen, the untouchable — basically, it's a leap of faith.

Trusting the unseen usually requires trusting our instincts, but if we are first trying to *find* our instincts, then in the meanwhile we have to trust others for whom we have respect. Letting go is a hard exercise because at times it feels like a life-

and-death struggle, giving up what's familiar for something that's unknown. Often we choose the former until the pain is so intense, we surrender and seek help. Our healthy side finally gets a chance to be heard and seen — and to survive.

Often our attachments define in part who we are, whether they are healthy or not (which is a whole other topic). Our primary identity is entwined with those relationships — those with too much debt, the constant need to feel less than, the fear of the unknown, and unresolved anger.

> ***The whole point is that we are the pioneers of our own journey. Of course it's scary; it's uncharted territory for us. But that's where growth and healing occur.***

How do we go from being a prisoner to a pioneer? Remember when you got a cut on your hand and you used Band-Aids until the time came to allow air and light to heal it? You removed the Band-Aid and it healed faster. Up until now, you have been an observer. Others have gone before you and have done exactly what you are doing. They have written books, run seminars, all giving testimony that they are experts in their field. Now you get to be the protagonist — the actual participant who is going to take the risks and reap the rewards.

TRUST:
A LEAP OF FAITH

Trust is believing in the intangible — a leap of faith. *Webster's* defines it as "reliance on the future truth of someone or something." It's the willingness to suspend control over something you usually don't have control over anyway. Trust is based upon being authentic and really knowing yourself and believing in your own competence.

In my first session with a new client, I usually ask that person to define "trust" and then ask how much that person trusts the people in his or her inner circle. Trust goes beyond believing that our partner is monogamous — it includes believing that our partner's feelings and words are concentric. It also includes knowing that someone will show up in an emergency for you. But do any of these people always tell you the truth? I ask clients to rate the people in their lives on a scale from 1 to 100%, 100% being most trustworthy. Most trustworthy means being 100% authentic.

We use this benchmark as a reference point as we move through the 20 topics in our sessions, to demonstrate where their lack of stability was reinforced, and how that showed up later in their lives as not being able to trust themselves.

If your early childhood years were chaotic, filled with consistent, unpredictable behavior by your caregivers whose words and actions were not congruent, you grew up in an environment that challenged your instincts and eroded your self-confidence. How often I have heard: "My father told me what I felt, and would argue with me if I disagreed." That dismissal of a young child's feelings is a trigger for the child to have self-esteem issues that manifest in her adult life as a lack of self-trust.

Kenny

Kenny had a twin brother who was shy. His parents always insisted he take his brother everywhere he went, which made Kenny angry. He never had his own life, and the family's attitude that Ronnie, the twin, was weak further enabled Ronnie to continue to act weak and be a victim.

Their mother never saw the boys as being different from each other. Her need to have them act close was just that — an act. Because there was no real individualization for each boy, the boys grew up always angry with each other, and to this day they are impatient with and hostile toward each other. But in the company of other people, they never show their disdain for one another. They put on their adapted personas.

The boys do not trust one another because they never learned to trust themselves. When a child is celebrated for being separate and is respected for being himself, trust can grow. A child who is not given support and not heard for being different grows up wary and suspicious of others.

It's no surprise that today Kenny has distorted behavior about money. He feels he never gets paid enough, purchases things he cannot afford and complains to his wife that she needs to go back to work while managing a household of three children, all under the age of ten.

Trusting yourself is a sign of true meaning and healing. How do you reach the goal of inner trust and self-love? Once again, you begin the process with baby steps. You need to establish respect for yourself. Keep your self-commitments, and respect will follow. Once there's respect, trust will endure.

> ***Commit to something — anything — and do it every day. Watch how the world does not stop spinning. Everybody goes about their lives doing what they do — and so can you.***

Then expand the commitment, add another task, follow the formula, continue to do it EVERY DAY. It will be a new positive habit, and the day you legitimately cannot do that thing, you will not feel guilty. You will feel in control and calm. You will have confidence that you can pick it up again tomorrow.

Anytime you promise to do something for yourself (make your bed, exercise, journal, avoid sugar, drink less) and then you do *not* do it, your inner five-year old is driving the bus, she has control. When you start to trust yourself, you are getting closer to your authentic self, increment-by-increment, rung-by-rung.

INTIMACY:
THE CLUB WE ALL WANT TO BELONG TO

Intimacy is learned at birth. As you've learned in these chapters, the first eight to ten months of an infant's life is a critical building block of time in his or her self-esteem and ability to trust. The "good enough" mother will hold her infant to her warmth constantly and be able to anticipate the needs of her child. That need and appropriate expectation signals to the newborn: "Someone knows what I want and gives it to me the second I need it. I feel safe."

Intimacy is one of those words that most people associate with sex. For me, it's about being real, visible in that nanosecond, and totally exposed for how I feel in that moment. It is a bond between you and another person — whether it's spiritual, physical, emotional, financial, or sexual. Having nothing to do with boundaries, it's where merging takes place — in the moment.

This is scary territory for people who live their lives on two tracks. The last thing they want to be is visible. Hiding is safe, disguises bring comfort, and shrouds throw off the enemy.

> **Here's a reality check:**
> **You cannot be truly intimate with someone else unless you are intimate with yourself first.**

You can have the illusion of closeness, but inside you know the real scoop. In many situations, you are there 90%, and the other 10% you keep in a safe place until you are ready to take that huge leap. You are holding on to what you think is some tiny shred of dignity and protection. Fear keeps you in check.

Sometimes intimacy is about feeling vulnerable and asking for what you need or want without trying to control the future. Intimacy with your self is being totally honest and accountable to yourself.

Lack of intimacy is more common than not; it's easier to turn one's eyes away than stand steadfast and clear with another person in the same split second.

There is only way out of this tunnel. The vehicle that will take you there is called trusting yourself. And the way to gain trust is to respect yourself, which automatically sets boundaries for the rest of the outside world. Once you start treating yourself with respect, you get to give yourself permission about what and whom you want close to your soul, and with whom you want to share your inner light. And as you let those certain people or events in, your heart expands, and joy becomes the order of the day.

MARGO

Margo was adopted, and her parents had two children after her. Her parents were very rigid, structured and terrified of life. Everything natural made her parents uncomfortable. They were not affectionate with each other, or with the children. Any physical contact made them pull away.

Physical contact is a primal need. Robbing a child of that tactile experience creates strong signals of not being wanted. It can lead a child to believe that "something is wrong with me." Physical closeness, skin to skin, is organic and feels good to both parties if they allow it to be so. Children are sensitive and perceptive so they can sense tightness in their parents, siblings and anyone around them.

That lack of physical intimacy became an issue as Margo got older. She had boyfriends very early, and sex before she was 16 years old. She was starved for affection. Her need for confirmation of her feelings was derailed very early, so her life continued to be split onto two tracks.

When she was in her 20s, she became a workaholic and a marathon runner. Literally and symbolically, she was running from the pain, numbing herself by working long hours and running endlessly. On the surface, she appeared intact financially. She made a good living and lived in a lovely home. She dated infrequently because she was so busy, or so she said. But the truth was that she felt out of control with other people, and more in control when she was alone. She expressed her angst by feeling she never earned enough money, so she kept working harder and harder as if she would someday feel content. The money had become her lover. But she was terrified of losing what assets she had. She could not sleep without a pill, could not relax, and could not be truly still.

One day, she was in a car accident and broke her collarbone, leg and arm. She was housebound for six months. Ironically, this was a true gift from the universe. She was forced to be still. This is when we started our work together and she set out on the path of seeking answers to the questions she never before had permission to express. She read books that had sat on her shelves never opened, asked spiritual questions from people she barely knew, and started to let others in. She experienced herself from another perspective and saw that she was able to not only survive sharing her long hidden shame about not feeling wanted, but her life began to feel slightly lighter, easier and less frightening.

As she let go and came to understand where her fear of intimacy had come from and how to manage it, she started to shift and heal. She was beginning to comprehend that she had to first be intimate with herself before being able to truly connect with another person.

Knowing herself on an intimate level established trust from within and grounded her. From that center, respect emanated. How she felt about money, and then how she handled it, shifted so that she no longer felt afraid of losing her assets. She is now enjoying the benefits of financial security, finally, and of having new friends who see her for who she is and value her.

Forgiving:
The Handmaiden of Trust

On our journey of healing, we come to many crossroads of opportunities. That's the whole purpose of choice: Do we pick the red door or the blue door? For the poet Robert Frost, the road less taken ended up being the right one. Sometimes, the road we pick is bumpy, full of fallen trees and brambles, and requires patience and compassion to keep going. Sometimes the one we pick is slippery and causes pain in every step, but we still keep going, even though, at the end of that journey, we may be full of regret and smack ourselves in the forehead asking, "What was I thinking?"

- How do we ask for forgiveness?
- From where do we dig deep to explain and humble ourselves for missing the obvious?
- How do we forgive another who has hurt us?
- From where do we dig deep to find the capacity to let go of the pain and anger to allow that person back in?

The Ultimate Goal

Asking ourselves these questions is a great first step in our process. Forgiving is a handmaiden of trust. Without her moving the pieces around on the board, trust can never return; and without trust, we cannot love.

- What value does it bring to not trust?
- Whose needs are getting met by not forgiving?
- What is protected when we don't forgive?

The need not to forgive sits on the mantel of not letting go. Forgiveness is about *giving*. Healthy relationships are based on forgiveness, which is the cornerstone of healing. It's about how to shift from being the victim who withholds to becoming the loving one who is open. Isn't that the person you want to be? It's not about condoning what the other person has done. It is about reconciliation. The act of forgiveness sits on high ground.

Afterword

There is no doubt that I am the fly in the ointment for many therapists and coaches. As Dr. Ditta Oliker, my former therapist, warned me 23 years ago: "You are the child in *The Emperor's New Clothes*, always stating what is obvious to you but obscure to the person you are talking with. You risk alienating those who would prefer to remain in the shadows and maintain status quo."

Arrogant and grandiose as this sounds, if you know yourself, you know mankind. We are all the same at our cores, wanting love, to feel connected and valued for who we are.

We all start at the same place — one of abandonment in those early years — and can end in the same place if we have chosen a life of self-awareness, joy, contentment and feeling whole. It's those years in between that challenge us and make us different; we are born unique but learn to mask who we really are.

This book is a written demonstration of my journey of healing; to have come from an emotionally challenged environment, living a life of detachment on two parallel tracks, to living on a single track of wholeness and contentment. To finally understand what love is, how to receive it and learning how to give it has taken me a lifetime. But it doesn't matter *when* we arrive, only that we *do* arrive.

My hope was to take you on my journey of healing, by starting with identifying feelings that may describe where you are today when you are reading this book, giving you definitions in every essay that I hope have helped you gain clarity of thought. And what triggers those feelings?

Then, we talked about how your emotions sit underneath those feelings and how interacting with others will fuel those emotions.

Next, you were offered four examples of behaviors that I know you have experienced but maybe never identified in a crystal clear way. But behaviors are clues; they point toward the source. It's our choice as adults to choose a different behavior.

Why did you pick up this book? For answers, for tools. Everybody wants to know how to fix his or her problems. I have addressed behaviors that you can use to shift the current way you manage your children, your significant other, and your finances. Remember, those are all collateral issues; they are the result of how the kinds of choices you made in the past don't really help you

Afterword

now. You can reclaim your power and make choices that suit you better and support your desire to be whole, so that you no longer have to live on two tracks.

Finally, you were offered an additional tool, *forgiveness*, which is part of letting go, a part of *healing*, the continuous process we have chosen to embrace. It is the balm we smooth on when faced with challenging circumstances.

Trust and *intimacy* are the goals this entire journey. They are the destination without the spa. When we finally reach the plateau where they are, we then get to see the road ahead and feel confident that we will manage it well, which will enable us to fully enjoy our lives.

> **Welcome home. You are the one you've been waiting for.**

SOME NOTES ABOUT HOW I GOT HERE

In the seventh grade, I wrote my first book, *The Muddy Days of Moppy Moss*. It never made it to Amazon. Charming as my mother found it, her encouragements went unheeded.

Some fifty odd years later I wrote *A Mother's Guide to Teaching Her Child How to Manage Money*, and *What Every Woman Needs to Understand About Getting a Mortgage*. More books that stayed under the radar. What happened in between those years is how I came to write this book, which is standing in the full light of day, totally visible, in your hands.

My career took a sharp turn in 2004, while I was attending a charitable event in Los Angeles. I met a woman who owned a women's clothing company that produced custom-fit upscale knitwear. The manufacturing business was completely foreign to me, and I loved the idea of taking on the challenge of learning a new industry. When she offered me a job as vice president of national sales, I gladly accepted.

The company's business model was unique; it was owned by a woman, an all-female staff manufactured the garments, and all the members of the national sales team were women. Since the clothing was also designed only for women, the entire client base was also female. It was during my time in this environment that I began to understand the unique intricacies of how women communicate, grow, and interact with each other. It was a truly intimate, eye-opening experience for me.

I witnessed many customers spending money they didn't have on things they really didn't need. I did not yet allow myself to see myself in their army. Self-denial kept me at a safe distance.

The company closed its doors after 27 years. While searching for a new career, my husband at the time suggested I might do well as a mortgage broker — a position in which the relationship with clients is rooted in trust.

I started the mortgage company, Home Loans for Women, and, once again, was amazed at the ways so many women had mismanaged their finances. The trusting relationships I developed with these women also afforded me much deeper insight into the intimate details of their lives, and I learned that many of them were coming out of abusive relationships. They were burdened with house payments they couldn't afford, and had children to feed, but were not receiving any financial support from their estranged husbands.

As I took them through the financing curve, I was basically educating them about the mortgage process, so I turned my tutorial into the books mentioned previously. The rumblings of my financial denial started to get increasingly louder. When it hit Mach I, I could no longer pretend I did not have my own financial issues. My behavior was tangled up with shame, fear, anger, self-sabotage, and depression.

I felt like a fraud most of my life, but right in front of me, my 11-year marriage was coming apart, I was jobless, our rental unit was being sold, my favorite dog was dying, and a lawsuit I had instigated was not settled yet. I was going down for the count, or so I thought.

It was at that turning point that my life started to shift big-time. I was being forced to get real, become accountable to myself, and rescue myself. I was being compelled to come out of the shadows, into the glaring light of choice and authenticity. It started an amazing journey, which then gave me rich insights that created this book, which is now sold on Amazon. Better late than never, Mother.

I have spent an enormous amount of time communicating with hundreds of women during the past five years. Ironically, as I learned about them, I was learning about myself; each of them held a small kernel of who I was. As they healed, so did I.

Painful as these past five years have been, they were my right of passage into ownership of my soul.

If I can do it, so can you. This is why I wrote the book: to give you permission, encouragement and tools to reclaim your soul and, to paraphrase Dr. Oliker, "to reclaim your lost childhood."

Suggested Readings

Aron, Elaine N. *The Highly Sensitive Person in Love.* Portland, OR: Broadway Books, 2000.

Baer, Heidi. *Har-money. Secrets to Lifelong Prosperity.* Treasure Island Press, 2005, http://treasureislandpress.com.

Brown, Brené C. *The Gifts of Imperfection.* Center City, MN: Hazelden, 2010.

Cameron, Julia. *The Artist's Way: A Spiritual Path to Higher Creativity.* New York, NY: G.P. Putnam's Sons, 1992.

Campbell, Chellie. *Zero to Zillionaire: 8 Foolproof Steps to Financial Peace of Mind* Naperville, IL: Sourcebooks, 2006.

Daily Om, newsletter: http://www.dailyom.com/cgi-bin/userinfo/settings.cgi

Friday, Nancy. *My Mother/Myself.* New York, NY: Delacorte Press, 1977.

Kindlon, Dan & Michael Thompson. *Raising Cain: Protecting the Emotional Life of Boys*. New York, NY: Ballantine Books 1999.

Kluger, Jeffrey. How Your Siblings Make You Who You Are, *Time*, July 10 2006.

Marano, Hara Estroff. Siblings...How They Really Shape You. *Psychology Today*, August 2010.

Miller, Alice. *The Drama of the Gifted Child: The Search For the True Self*. New York, NY: Basic Books, 1997.

Oliker, Ditta M. *The Light Side of the Moon: Reclaiming Your Lost Potential*. Central Recovery Press, Fall 2012. Originally published as *Hide and Seek: Reclaiming Childhood's Lost Potential*, 2010.

Piver, Susan. *How Not to Be Afraid of Your Own Life*. New York, NY: St. Martin's Press, 2007.